I0800110

Praise for
Surrendering Certainty

"Reading *Surrendering Certainty* helped dispel all my fearful thoughts about taking the wrong next step and ruining my life. Abby invites her reader to ask the right questions and rest in our heavenly Father's certain faithfulness. Every chapter is grounded in biblical wisdom and provides practical guidance so that even indecisive people like me can make well-informed choices and move forward with confident faith."

—**Lyli Dunbar,** biblical life coach, host of *The Wildfire Faith* podcast, and writer for Love God Greatly and Proverbs 31 Ministries' First 5 app

"Abby McDonald writes with the warmth of a trusted friend and the wisdom of someone who has wrestled with the same doubts and fears we all face. *Surrendering Certainty* will have you laughing, reflecting, and learning to recognize God's gentle guidance in the everyday. Through her own story, Abby invites readers to release the need for control, embrace the freedom of faith, and take the next step—no matter how uncertain it feels. If you're longing to hear God's voice and trust his plan, this book is a must-read."

—**Krissy Nelson,** author, speaker, author coach, Krissy Nelson Consulting

"In *Surrendering Certainty,* Abby McDonald helps us discover true contentment in our right-now moments through surrendering to God our need for next-step certainty. McDonald beautifully weaves engaging personal stories and solid biblical truths throughout the pages, showing us how to release our expectations for the clarity we think we need and embrace the journey of moving forward in faith. Readers will appreciate the simple yet practical steps to walk forward without fear, trade comfort and familiarity for adventurous faith, and consider the possibility that life's distractions are, as McDonald suggests, 'holy moments' meant to refine us and transform our lives. I highly recommend *Surrendering Certainty*—a message that reminds us our purpose and calling are ultimately rooted in Jesus. This book will refresh your soul and encourage you to venture beyond whatever you're waiting for."

—**Doris Swift,** host of the *Fierce Calling* podcast, speaker, and author of *Surrender the Joy Stealers*

"When it comes to following God's plan for our lives, we often want to know exactly what the future holds, along with step-by-step instructions for how to make it happen. However, as Abby points out in *Surrendering Certainty*, hearing from God is less about future outcomes and more about present peace and obedience. If you're stuck—craving security, paralyzed with fear, worried about making the wrong choice, or doubting your ability to fulfill God's call—this book provides a wise and thoughtful way forward. By asking probing questions, sharing personal struggles, and drawing truth from scripture, Abby helps us see that trusting God for the next step is what brings true freedom."

—**Lois Flowers,** blogger, editor, and self-described person who always reads the end of the book first

"Hearing and heeding the voice of God is the surest way I know to turn a weary faith walk into a wide-eyed adventure. That's why I'm thankful for the message of *Surrendering Certainty*. With the warmth of a friend and the wisdom of a mentor, Abby McDonald demystifies the idea of hearing from God and equips us to be confident listeners and courageous followers. If you're ready for an adventure, open this book and offer God your ears."

—**Alicia Bruxvoort,** author, Bible teacher, member of the Proverbs 31 Ministries writing team

"This book is for anyone who thinks knowing God's voice so as to understand his guidance is either too murky or reserved for a spiritually select few. *Surrendering Certainty* unpacks practical, scripture-based insight to help us get unstuck and go where God leads. After watching Abby absolutely live out this book navigating big moves, career opportunities, and frustrating obstacles, I'm thrilled her tested wisdom is here for us all."

—**Lisa Appelo,** author of *Life Can Be Good Again: Putting Your World Back Together After It All Falls Apart*

surrendering certainty

surrendering certainty

HEARING GOD TODAY BY LETTING GO OF TOMORROW

Abby McDonald

LEAFWOOD
PUBLISHERS
an imprint of Abilene Christian University Press

SURRENDERING CERTAINTY

Hearing God Today by Letting Go of Tomorrow

LEAFWOOD PUBLISHERS
an imprint of Abilene Christian University Press

ISBN 978-1-68426-183-3

Printed in the United States of America

Published in association with The Blythe Daniel Agency, Inc., PO Box 64197, Colorado Springs, CO 80962.

Cataloging-in-Publication Data is on file at the Library of Congress, Washington, DC.

Cover design by Greg Jackson, Thinkpen Design
Interior text design by Sandy Armstrong, Strong Design

Leafwood Publishers is an imprint of Abilene Christian University Press
ACU Box 29138
Abilene, Texas 79699

1-877-816-4455
www.leafwoodpublishers.com

26 27 28 29 30 31 / 7 6 5 4 3 2

To Jaden, Gabe, and Elise—

Every day you teach me what it means
to hear his voice
and respond in faith.
I'm so grateful to be your mama.

contents

introduction

When my husband and I were newlyweds, we developed a saying for God-moments when his leading was unmistakable. We called them *two-by-fours to the head*. I realize this description doesn't sound very pleasant, but if you've had one of these moments before, you know. You're praying to God, asking for his leading, and you've probably even missed a few of his nudges. Lord knows I have. But our God is patient. He's not giving up on us. Then, a series of events, conversations, or situations makes his guidance so obvious you would have to be completely oblivious to miss it.

Sometimes these moments come in the form of a phone call at the exact right time, answering a question like, "Do I take the job?" Other times, it may be a text message from a friend you haven't talked to about your desire to pursue a specific ministry, but somehow, they know. "I think you'd be really good at this," the message says. The message points you to an opportunity in line with what you've hoped for in secret. "You should go for it." These moments make us stop and thank God for his direction.

They're what our hearts long for because, deep down, we want to know we're on the right path.

During our first year of marriage, my husband and I received several of these distinct two-by-four moments. We sought God's guidance in some major decisions, and he gave it in ways we couldn't miss. Although some of the life changes he led us toward were difficult, he reassured us with unmistakable evidence of his leading. When we made two cross-country moves within the first five years of marriage, we needed those confirmations. And God knew this. Even when we encountered bumps in the road, we didn't question the initial green light he gave us.

Now my husband and I have been married for eighteen years. And while we still occasionally have those two-by-four moments, they're fewer and farther between. Yes, God gives us confirmations, but they often happen after we've taken the step of faith, not before. We see the proof of his mercies in hindsight, and his leading looks more like gentle taps than whacks with huge pieces of wood. There's a lot more seeking and faltering through the dark, and the soles of my shoes are worn from prayer walks with our dog.

What changed? Our faith? While every spiritual journey has its ups and downs, the Author of our faith is constant. No, what changed is our time on the adventure. God is growing us up, and he doesn't want our faith to stay in one place. As we move with him, he asks us to trust him with a little bit more, challenges us in new ways, and continues to ask the lifelong question, "Will you come with me?" This question often comes in the form of a love tap; one we may not even recognize until we've spent time fostering our ability to do so.

I'd love to tell you I'm an expert at recognizing those taps. But more often than I care to admit, I question God's voice rather than act on it. I hesitate and make excuses about why what I *think* he's asking me to do isn't possible. Hearing him and responding to him is a lifelong process in which I continue to learn, be challenged, falter, and get back up again. And the more I know him, the more I realize how much more there is to know.

If you'd told me five years ago I was going to write a book about hearing God's voice, I would've said you were crazy. I would've said there were a million people more qualified to speak on such a topic and given you a long list of reasons why writing this book wasn't possible. But over the past two years, I've learned that when God gives you a message to share, it becomes like a slow-burning flame. You can try to let the wick reach its endpoint, but it keeps burning with its steady, persistent heat. As much as I tried to evade his prompting to share this book, I knew it was one I had to write.

Each week, I talk to people who feel stuck in their spiritual walks. They're asking age-old questions like, "Is this God's voice? Is it God's will? How do I know?" I know the angst and the frustration behind these questions because I've asked them myself. I know what it's like to spend more time thinking about my next move than making it. But this is not the life God wants us to live. He did not create us and name us to live lives where we remain stagnant, held in a listless cycle of doubt and inertia.

Reader, if you're holding this book right now, I've prayed for you. I've prayed that the words flowing on this page will ignite within you a desire to follow God that exceeds your desire for signs and writings on the wall. I've prayed that as you read, you will know and receive the gift he gives to each and every one of us who call him Lord: the ability to hear his voice.

In the pages ahead, we will unpack one of the biggest lies followers of Jesus believe about hearing and responding to the voice of God: that we need certainty. And friends, I'm not talking about eternity here. I'm talking about certainty in this life, here on this planet. Certainty in what Paul calls *seen* and *temporary* (2 Cor. 4:18). We think we need a list of guarantees about the outcome, telling us what's on the other side of our obedience. It's the reason why we ask for one more sign, one more confirmation, and one more peek into the future. It's the reason why we either fail to recognize God's voice or don't act on it. And because we believe this lie, we often miss out on the big, beautiful life God has for us, never pursuing the nudges he gives us or the dreams he places within our hearts.

As we unpack the varying facets of this lie, we will study three truths Jesus states about his followers in John 10:

1. My sheep hear my voice (v. 27).
2. They will come, go, and find pasture (v. 9).
3. No one will snatch them out of my Father's hand (vv. 28–29).

These truths will become our foundation as we learn how to recognize God's voice, respond to it, and act without fear. Through these pages, we will see how these truths are the guarantees our hearts long for, and they far exceed any guarantee this life has to offer. Instead of chasing temporary security that fades and never satisfies, we will move forward in the only true source of safety: our Father's embrace.

Are you ready? I can't wait to take this journey with you. Grab your favorite caffeinated beverage, and let's go.

PART ONE

YOU KNOW HIS VOICE

"My sheep listen to my voice;
I know them, and they follow me."

John 10:27

1

open the door to a future you can't see

Wait a minute. He can't be serious.

With no notice, my first ride on a motorcycle became a test of faith in my husband's driving ability and more of an adventure than I had anticipated. He headed toward North Ogden Canyon, Utah, and within seconds, we climbed hundreds of feet above the valley below, its expanse stretching out behind us.

Lord Jesus, I really love the life you've given me and our beautiful son. I don't want to careen off a cliff today.

I envisioned those donkeys who carry people along the edge of the Grand Canyon with their riders' feet dangling inches from the massive, fatal drop. I had always thought those people must have a screw loose, and yet here I was, buzzing along the highway at a speed much faster than a donkey with the precipice to my right getting higher by the second. Cars whipped past us in the other lane, seeming closer without the protection of glass and metal around me. I fixed my gaze straight ahead and clasped Chris's waist tighter as the wind pressed against my leather jacket. *Why is he taking this route? Has he lost his mind?*

I knew God had prompted me to climb on this bike with my husband, but I didn't know why. And now I was questioning my judgment.

After a few minutes, I realized shouting was no use, so I settled against the backrest and tried to relax. We finally reached the flat part of the road, and the canyon faded behind us. Soon we were surrounded by evergreen trees and a lush green landscape with mountains towering around us in every direction. Chris rolled the throttle as we entered a new town. Its welcome sign read "Eden," and I drank in its beauty like a fresh glass of water. Sunlight bathed us on each side, and a full grin spread across my face, fed by adrenaline and wonder. We explored Eden for an hour, and I sighed with relief as I noticed my husband had picked a different route home.

By the time we pulled into the driveway, I was craving more. I was not the same Abby who had climbed on the bike an hour before. But first, I made sure my husband knew he nearly gave me a heart attack.

"The canyon? Really?"

Chris smiled and shrugged. "I wanted to break you in quick," he said.

"By making me think I was going to die?"

He laughed and assured me of his driving ability. After talking and chuckling for several minutes, we went into our friends' house to pick up our son.

This ride was the first of many my husband and I took together during the decade he owned a motorcycle. He always drove, and I sat passenger, taking in the sights and sounds around me with each bend revealing something new. Although that first route wasn't one I would've chosen, it mirrors my faith in many ways. While I chase certainty and control, God beckons me to trust. He invites me to come with him, propelled by my faith and my knowledge of his character more than my need to know what's ahead.

More times than I care to admit, I sense his nudge or his prompting, but I stall. Instead of moving, I ask for a sign. And then another one, and another, until my asking becomes an endless loop and quest for information. I tell myself this inaction and hesitation is because I want to make sure it's God I'm hearing; but if I'm honest, my motivation is more like fear. Fear of the unknown. Fear of looking foolish.

What I can't see keeps me from accepting God's invitation, from believing he has a reason for giving it. To receive the gift, my faith in the middle of the unknown must outweigh my fear of uncertainty. Even if just for a moment.

What if this belief is the key to more than surviving motorcycle rides along massive rock cliffs? What if it's the key to unlocking the life God has for us? To hear his voice in our everyday experiences and act on it? Often, we receive a word from God but we spend more time questioning it than responding to it. We ask ourselves questions like, "Was that really God or just my imagination?" Or, "If that was really God, why does this situation look completely different than I envisioned?"

These questions can keep us stuck in a pattern of doubt for months or even years. We want assurance that we're acting on God's voice rather than our own motives, and sometimes the assurance we seek doesn't come. Or if it does, it looks different from what we anticipated. We may not even recognize it.

What if God has already given us everything we need to recognize his voice? What if the certainty we long for has been given to us but we're overlooking it?

If we look at the history of humanity, we see a pattern. Questions about what God did or didn't say aren't new. These questions started in the garden of Eden. But it wasn't Adam or Eve who originally asked them. It was Satan. The question he asked Eve changed not only our relationship with God but our connection with him: "Did God really say . . . ?" (Gen. 3:1).

Of course, we know where this question led. Adam and Eve fell for the deception. But it also led to the perpetual questioning of God's voice, which still misleads us today. The Enemy continues to ask his original question, and it can change the trajectory of our lives.

While the Enemy can question, it's important to remember he can't read our minds. He is not omniscient like God. He and his armies operate through careful observation. When they spot a point of weakness like a questioning or doubtful mind, they pounce. They know it is an opportune time to thwart God's plans for our lives, and they make the most of it. This is what Satan did with Eve.

After Eve responded to Satan, he lied to her about what the outcome of her actions would be—"You will not surely die," he said (Gen. 3:4 ESV)—and then offered her something she couldn't refuse: knowledge.

> *When the woman saw that the fruit of the tree was good for food and pleasing to the eye, and also desirable for gaining wisdom, she took some and ate it. She also gave some to her husband, who was with her, and he ate it.* (Gen. 3:6)

The moment Eve chose to eat the fruit, she stopped trusting that God had given her the knowledge she needed for the day. She wanted more. Instead of believing God had a good reason for limiting her awareness, she believed she needed a higher level of understanding.

At this dividing point in history, Eve traded God's yoke for the Enemy's. And the Enemy's yoke says this: We need more information than what God chooses to give us. Trust is exchanged for a yearning for more knowledge. This same longing feeds our hesitation today.

A Different Kind of Yoke

I believe uncertainty is one of the reasons why the question, "Did God really say," is so effective. We long to see a map laid out before us with a clear path marked and assurance that we're headed in the right direction. We want his guidance to be as obvious as Siri when she tells us, "Make a U-turn." Sidenote: I honestly don't know how I ever survived driving in unfamiliar areas without this handy assistant. But God doesn't work this way. He wants us to live with a daily reliance on him and to enter a relationship where he is our friend, not our GPS.

When we're not mindful of how we respond to God, our desire for certainty becomes a yoke we carry. And this is exactly what our enemy wants. He knows if we're weighed down by this yoke that is too heavy for our finite bodies to carry, it will be more difficult for us to fulfill the plans God has for us. We can spend months or even years on an endless quest for knowledge, believing knowledge will give us freedom.

But here's the irony of it all: The more knowledge we obtain, the less freedom we feel. Instead of moving forward, unencumbered by an endless sea of information, we keep seeking more. Much like scrolling on the internet is an endless loop, we keep looking for more answers before we act.

Instead of offering us more information, Jesus offers us a different yoke. He tells us to come to him and to lay down all our what-ifs.

> *Come to me, all you who are weary and burdened, and I will give you rest. Take my yoke upon you and learn from me, for I am gentle and humble in heart, and you will find rest for your souls. For my yoke is easy and my burden is light.* (Matt. 11:28–30)

When most of us envision a yoke, we think of a burden. If you look up "yoke" in a thesaurus, "burden" is listed as one of its synonyms. It is a device joining together two animals, usually consisting of a crosspiece that encloses the head of the animal. By using this device, the work animals can carry loads more effectively. But if the yoke doesn't fit the animal and is too large or too small, it is useless.

Jesus used this analogy because he knew this imagery would be familiar to his disciples. He evokes a picture of an animal trying to carry a load that is ill-fitted for him. It's cumbersome and awkward. This is what we do when we try to run outside of the knowledge God gives us for today and into the future. We take up a yoke ill-suited for us. We're going back to the Garden, trying to obtain more awareness and power than we can carry.

Now, notice here when Jesus says his yoke is easy and his burden is light, he doesn't say our lives will be easy and light. Responding to his voice and being obedient doesn't mean our lives will be free of struggle or hardship; but he says he will give us what we need. He invites us to trade our worry about tomorrow for his presence today. He asks us to live with him at this moment, fully present in the gift of now.

The yoke is easy because I am focusing my energy on what God has given me right now instead of worrying about what he will give me tomorrow. His strength and grace for today. His love and friendship for today. When I trade this for the worries and stresses of the future, I've taken on a weight my soul can't carry. His voice in my life becomes muted because I'm racing into a time and place that hasn't occurred yet. My trust falters, and my perpetual search for more confirmation spirals. A finite mind and body can't carry the knowledge and weight of an infinite God. God is outside of time, but we aren't. Jesus is inviting me to trade all my stress about the future for the beauty right here in this moment. Is it easy? Heck no. But it's worth it. It's the same invitation he gives to each of us.

> A finite mind and body can't carry the knowledge and weight of an infinite God. God is outside of time, but we aren't.

Receiving the Gift

What is the key to exchanging this yoke of certainty for the freedom Jesus offers? Recognition. It is receiving the gift he gives to each one of his followers: the ability to hear his voice. This isn't a gift he reserves for a select few, like the person behind the pulpit or the woman who leads the Bible study at church. Every one of us who names Jesus as Lord is given this ability.

> *My sheep hear my voice, and I know them, and they follow me.* (John 10:27 ESV)

For many of us, this gift seems elusive or out of reach. I mean, sure God talked to the prophets of the Old Testament and the disciples in Acts, but does he still talk to us today?

According to this scripture, yes, he does. As a matter of fact, Jesus states this truth to the Pharisees not once but four times in this passage. The problem for the Pharisees? They aren't hearing it.

If there was ever a group of people who appeared to meet all the criteria needed to hear God, it was the Pharisees. They knew the law of Moses and followed it to a T. They spent the required time at the synagogue and kept the Sabbath. And yet, these people did not hear or recognize the voice of God when he was standing right in front of them, in the flesh. Their devotion to God was surface level, and Jesus knew this.

But there's another facet to the Pharisees' blindness and inability to hear God's voice. Of all the people Jesus spoke to in the Gospels, they're the ones we see make the most demands. Give us a sign, they say. If you're the Messiah, tell us plainly. They witness the same miracles and hear the same message everyone else does, and yet they fail to see that Jesus is the One they've been waiting for.

More than anyone else in the Gospels, the Pharisees illustrate this truth: More knowledge does not lead to more freedom. Their endless asking and demanding led them not toward the truth but further away from it. The yoke they carried was one of pride and an endless quest for information. In contrast, the person who recognizes the voice of God knows that without faith, it is impossible to please him. And faith requires responding to his voice without knowing what will happen on the other side of obedience. As William Paul Young writes, "Faith does not grow in the house of certainty."[1]

Instead of being led by pride, the person who hears God's voice knows there is nothing he or she can do to earn this gift. This mysterious gift is not a result of achieving some invisible rung on a totem pole of spirituality. It is given without reservation. But to activate its power, we must use it.

Saying Yes to the Unknown

Several months ago, I talked to a coaching friend who knew God was leading her in a new direction with her business. He prompted her through changing passions and circumstances to make a shift in the clients she served. This nudge began a year prior to our conversation, but instead of acting, she stalled. Why? Because she was unsure. She didn't know how her current clients would react or how others would perceive her. She worried that making the change would hurt her business rather than help it gain momentum, and this uncertainty kept her stuck in her head. Lord knows I have been there too. Anyone else?

The push to act came after spending three months on Zoom calls with other coaches who shared both their wins and their struggles. Each coach opened up about her fears and areas where she struggled, but each one also encouraged others to take steps forward. Even if it was scary.

Through these honest conversations, my friend realized not only that she wasn't alone but that she had everything she needed to move forward. She had the experience and expertise her clients needed. And more importantly, she had God leading her.

No, she didn't know how people would react to the change. None of us can predict or control the opinions of others. But the prospect of missing the opportunity to which God called her was no longer an option. She stepped into the unknown with the certainty that each misstep would lead her into a greater reliance on him. This leads us to another fear that keeps us stuck in a cycle of hesitation: the fear of failure.

If we're trying something new, this fear is guaranteed to make an appearance. And the more public our failures or missteps are, the more difficult it is to move past this fear. For example, if you're a content creator, a public figure, or a leader in your line of business, your work is on display for others to scrutinize and publicly comment on. Even if you're not in a line of work that's in the public eye, you probably have friends and family members you share life with. When you make a change, start a new job, or try a new endeavor, you want to share it with someone.

So what happens when we fail? What happens when the new thing we try doesn't work and everyone knows it? We remember the courage it took for us to try. Yes, that's right.

The truth is that if we're not making mistakes, we're not learning anything. Your first draft will be bad. Your first idea will flop. But if you don't take the first step, you'll never grasp what works and what doesn't. You'll never be able to tweak a process you don't start.

One of the aspects I love about the apostle Peter's story is the number of times he publicly failed. I know this statement might seem a bit harsh, but the reason why I love this characteristic of Peter's is because it reminds me God can still use me, even when I mess things up. Peter walked on water, but most of us remember him for sinking. Jesus called him the rock on which he would build his church, but most of us remember him for denying Jesus three times.

While the Gospels may show Peter as someone who abandoned Jesus at his weakest moment, Acts shows him as a completely different person. He isn't the scared fisherman for whom the rooster crows anymore. He is consumed with his passion to spread the Word of God, and nothing will stop him from telling everyone he encounters. Even death.

After the priests and temple guard threw Peter and John in jail for preaching about Jesus, the priests commanded them not to speak of Jesus any longer. They were alarmed by the growing number of people who were believing in Jesus and were desperate to put a stop to it. But Peter and John were not fearful or deterred, and responded by saying: "Which is right in God's eyes: to listen to you, or to him? You be the judges! As for us, we cannot help speaking about what we have seen and heard" (Acts 4:19–20).

Peter and John let the uncertainty of their situation propel them toward Jesus instead of away from him. They were clear about their purpose and their mission, and they would not let anyone stop them from completing it. So instead of cowering in fear over the priests' words, they proclaimed their commitment. They said yes to the unknown because the message they had to share was too good to keep to themselves.

Despite Peter and John's blunt refusal to stop talking about Jesus, the priests let them go. Peter and John went straight back to their people and reported everything that had happened to them, including the threats. Now, I imagine a report of such events during our current day and time would bring fear and uncertainty. If I were on the receiving end of their news, I would probably question God and beg for protection. But the early church's response was quite different.

Instead of letting fear overtake them, they worshiped. They prayed not for protection and an easy road but for boldness:

> *Now, Lord, consider their threats and enable your servants to speak your word with great boldness. Stretch out your hand to heal and perform signs and wonders through the name of your holy servant Jesus.*
> (Acts 4:29–30)

After this prayer, the place where they were meeting shook. They were given the Holy Spirit, and the boldness they asked for filled them to overflowing.

Here's the challenge I want to give you today: If you're afraid of the place God is leading you, let your fear propel you toward Jesus instead of away from him.

If others are telling you the vision you received or the step of faith you feel called to take is crazy, tell God about it. Your transparency with him will not only bring you into deeper intimacy with God but will allow him to transform your fear into fortitude. Like the disciples in Acts, we can have the boldness to do what God asks, even when others don't understand.

If you fail or falter like Peter, let your missteps push you into a deeper reliance on Jesus. Admit your shortcomings to him. Bring him your disappointments and your frustrations. When we try to hide these feelings from him, it creates a chasm between us and God. He cannot minister to a heart that's closed off from him. But when we come to him with our hurts, he brings peace that goes beyond our situation.

The Certainty We Have

When I climbed on the back of that motorcycle years ago, I was coming out of a long season of postpartum depression. My marriage had taken a hit as a result of three major life transitions in the span of one year, and I was at a loss for what to do. As crazy as it sounds, this invitation from my husband felt like God was reaching out his hand toward me, asking me to take hold. Most of the time in the past, my mind would have responded with something cynical like, "Yeah, but will he catch me?" But in that moment, God broke through my walls of cynicism and brought me straight to his heart. I saw him standing there, loving me. He wanted nothing more than for me to admit my need, but he also knew I was afraid.

I'm so glad I didn't let fear keep me standing in the yard, watching my husband drive away. Instead, I said yes to the uncertainty. I climbed on the back of the bike, not knowing what the adventure would bring but knowing God had a reason for it. And after that ride, we were changed. My husband and I formed a new bond. There would still be hard days, and the struggle didn't vanish. But I knew I wasn't alone in it, and this truth made all the difference.

This is the certainty we have when we step into the unknown: Jesus is applauding in heaven, saying, "Yes, my child. You can step into the uncertainty without fear because I am already there. I am on the other side of the future you can't see yet. You can move forward even if you're afraid because I will never shame you or disown you."

When we decide to respond to something God calls us to do with a yes, he is always for us. And each time we move forward in faith, we are made more perfect in his love.

DISCUSSION QUESTIONS

1. Has there ever been a time in your life when you felt God prompting you to take a step of faith but you stalled because you wanted more information? As you gained more information, did it give clarity or have the opposite effect?

2. Right before Eve ate the fruit, she observed it and determined that it "was desirable for gaining wisdom" (Gen. 3:6). What do you think is so appealing about knowledge that it made the first man and woman sin against God?

3. What do you think it would look like to let your fear propel you toward Jesus instead of away from him? Has there been a time in your life when you did this? What was the result?

2

God wants you to say yes

"Will it hurt you?"

My parents tell me I asked this question as a toddler whenever I tried something new or unfamiliar. The fear that a new endeavor would cause physical harm was prevalent and often kept me from taking risks. Although I don't know whether this fear originated from an actual accident or from my parents' reactions to things, my own kids' behavior sometimes gives me clues.

When my firstborn learned to ride a bike without training wheels, I saw a similar pattern. Once he was aware he might fall, he made every excuse he could think of not to try. The bike was too big. His legs were too tired. But when pressed to be honest, the truth came out. He was afraid.

My mind often goes to the same place as my son's when God prompts me to take a risk. Until several years ago, I didn't realize what the root of my fear was. I was afraid of being punished. Although I didn't see it for many years as a new believer, my reasoning went something like this: If I try this new thing and fall, God will punish me. If I don't get it right the first time and I falter, he'll never ask me to do anything for him again.

If fear of punishment from God doesn't derail me, another fear takes over. After taking steps of faith and saying yes to God in my own imperfect way, I noticed something. When we say yes to God, we become a target for the Enemy. He doesn't want our obedience and would rather we stay stagnant in our lives and our purpose.

I remember one season when my husband and I prayed over a big life decision that would require us to uproot our family, rent out our home in an upside-down economy, and move cross-country. All of the arrows pointed toward taking this crazy, life-altering step, and we took it. But for months afterward, we encountered one difficulty after another.

Although my spirit questioned God, I don't ever remember questioning him out loud or in my prayers. However, this period of my life and others like it caused me to see that the boldness of our faith often correlates to the amount of spiritual warfare we encounter. And if I'm honest, part of me wants to shrink back whenever I feel the pull to be audacious and brave for God. I know if I'm sitting on the sofa eating potato chips, I'm much less likely to become an enemy target. But as much as I love carbs, I don't want to miss the life God is leading me toward.

Perhaps you can relate? We're like Peter, standing at the edge of the boat. Our heart beckons us to step out onto the water and take God's hand. But then we remember—Peter sank. We remember how the Enemy asked to sift through him like wheat. And then he did. The times we sank in the past rise to the surface of our minds, and our fear of the water becomes our focus instead of God's gaze. So we decide to stay put. The prospect of failure is too great.

This is the type of dialogue I've had in my mind more times than I can count. I've reasoned myself to death, and I'm sure I've missed opportunities for God to work in me and through me.

There is another type of fear that can arise when we feel prompted to do something new or unfamiliar. We touched on it a bit in the last chapter, and it's fear of people. We're afraid others will talk and point out our inadequacies. Sometimes these people are only in our heads, but other times real, vocal influencers in our lives speak their opinions. They tell us to stick with what's safe and familiar. They ask questions like, "What if it doesn't work out?"

No matter what type of fear we're facing, God's Word speaks to each and every one of them. He knew we would be afraid, and this is why the Bible has over 365 commands saying, "Do not be afraid." These words are more of a reassurance than a reprimand and are intended to keep our focus on the One who knows what's on the other side of our yes.

Several years ago, I went through a season where I felt stuck in a continual state of doubt and apprehension. There were steps I felt God prompting me to take in my writing and my ministry, but I was paralyzed by what I couldn't see. Each of these types of fears we discussed surfaced at one point or another. In his grace, God opened my eyes to these words found in 1 John. These are familiar verses, and I'd read them many times, but God brought them to life in a new way. In this letter to the church, John says: "There is no fear in love. But perfect love drives out fear, because fear has to do with punishment. The one who fears is not made perfect in love" (1 John 4:18).

Identifying the Trigger Point

For years, I didn't understand this verse. It seemed as though God was holding us to an impossible standard. Not fear? God gave us our emotions, right? And isn't fear one of the emotions he created us to feel?

While it is unrealistic for us to think we'll ever live a life free from fear, it's important to realize God gave us this emotion as an indicator. It is a warning light alerting us to potential harm; so the key question we need to ask ourselves is, what is the warning light pointing to?

Here are three common trigger points to which fear often draws an arrow:

1. A past trauma we haven't dealt with
2. An insecurity we need to surrender to the Lord
3. A desire to see a future God hasn't yet revealed to us

In each circumstance, there is heart work involved. For the first trigger point, we may need to see a counselor and deal with the pain we've tried to keep buried. Because buried pain and trauma will always resurface later, even if we think we've moved past it.

The second trigger is more common, and one I've dealt with many times. I try to place my security in places it doesn't belong, like validation from others or an outcome that unfolds exactly how I envisioned it. But the longer I walk with Jesus, the more I see the truth: This type of security is fleeting, and it never satisfies.

While the third trigger overlaps with the second, it can often disguise itself with good intentions. We may dismiss our desire to see the future or our need for certainty, thinking we're just being responsible. We say things to ourselves like, "Doesn't God want us to produce good fruit? Doesn't he want to see a harvest?"

But here's the key aspect of obedience we forget: God alone is responsible for the fruit. Our responsibility is to plant the seeds (see 1 Cor. 3:7). When we focus all of our time and energy on obtaining a specific outcome on the outside, we forget the heart work that is taking place on the inside. God is growing us up and using us to help others grow, but this growth may not be outwardly visible. It takes time, and the process may be slower than we'd like. As author Madeleine L'Engle says, "We have to be braver than we think we can be, because God is constantly calling us to be more than we are."[1]

> When we focus all of our time and energy on obtaining a specific outcome on the outside, we forget the heart work that is taking place on the inside.

When we fear those steps of obedience needed for growth, we forget the nature of God. God will not punish us for doing something he's asked us to do. As we covered in Chapter One, each of us can hear his voice. One of the primary keys to fostering this ability is responding to it. Will the outcome always look the way we think it will? No, many times it won't. But when we move forward in faith anyway, we allow his love to propel us instead of our fear.

There is no fear in love because each time we move forward with love for God and others as our motivators, we can know he is for us.

A Perfect Love Mindset versus a Future Punishment Mindset

Now that we've identified some of the triggers our fear points to, we can unpack this verse from 1 John more. John tells us that perfect love drives out fear, but how do we live in this way? How do we live with a perfect love mindset rather than a future punishment mindset? In other words, how do we live in the truth of God's love rather than being motivated by a fear of judgment?

The key is found earlier in the chapter. John goes into great detail about how the believer is to live, and one of the first points he makes is to tell us to "test the spirits to see whether they are from God" (1 John 4:1). How do we know if a spirit is from God? If it acknowledges that Jesus Christ is the Son of God.

This identifier seems self-explanatory and almost too simple, but John doesn't stop there. He says spirits that are not from God "speak from the viewpoint of the world, and the world listens to them" (1 John 4:5). Ah, now we're getting somewhere. While John doesn't elaborate on what the viewpoint of the world means, I believe it's worth developing this idea further. Because in order to understand what a perfect love mindset means, we must first be able to identify those false spirits. Why? Because they're the ones who will point the arrow of our minds toward future punishment. Always.

If we take a look at the world around us, it doesn't take long to see the viewpoint of the world John talks about in this letter. But because it is everywhere, it can also be easy to become numb to it. We have to be alert and on our guard, or we can start following these world-centered viewpoints without even realizing it.

In this book's key passage, John 10, Jesus says his sheep follow his voice, but he also makes another distinction. He says his sheep will not follow a stranger. As a matter of fact, they will run away from one.

> *They will never follow a stranger; in fact, they will run away from him because they do not recognize a stranger's voice.* (John 10:5)

The more time we spend in this passage, the more it becomes apparent that these sheep have spent so much time with Jesus that following him is second nature. When they hear someone else who is trying to mimic his voice or lead them out of the safe pasture, they aren't fooled. Proximity to Jesus has brought an irreplaceable familiarity with his nature. It can't be copied. This closeness and level of safety with Jesus is what will keep us from following a stranger as well. When these world-centered viewpoints attempt to distract us from our home, we must remember who the true Shepherd is.

Recently, the Netflix series *All the Light We Cannot See* captured my interest. It is based on the Pulitzer Prize–winning novel by Anthony Doerr and follows the story of a blind French girl, Marie, during World War II. Using her uncle's radio transmitter, she sends coded messages for help to the Allies using braille readings of *Twenty Thousand Leagues Under the Sea*. Any type of radio broadcast during Nazi occupation is prohibited with a penalty of death, so Marie risks her life each time she turns on the radio. The voices of the world are loud, and they repeatedly tell her to abort her mission. They tell her to submit to her enemy.

One of the story's other key characters is a German orphan, Werner, who is skilled not only at repairing radios but also at finding the exact location of a broadcast. Once the Nazis realize his skill, he is recruited into their military against his will, and his training is fast-tracked. He enters France and his superior gives him one primary objective: Find the girl who is sending the radio messages each night.

But the more Werner listens to Marie's broadcasts, the more he realizes he can't place her life in jeopardy. Her broadcasts not only send signals to the Allies but give encouraging messages of hope to everyone listening, reminding them of their shared humanity. She reminds Werner of who he was before being recruited by the Nazis and that he still has a choice about whose voice to follow. Despite being German, he is disillusioned by his regime's complete disregard for human life. Even when he eventually traces the radio signal to Marie's uncle's house, he conceals the signal's existence once he sees Marie and realizes she is the one he's been listening to every evening.

As I watched each episode of this series, I was struck by Marie's and Werner's courage and belief in the power of hope. Even though Werner didn't know Marie, he felt connected to her. He chose love instead of focusing on the worst-case scenario, and because of his bravery, many lives were saved. And even though Marie knew she risked her life each time her radio light clicked on, she chose to focus on the possibility of hope instead of the voices of the world around her. Future punishment was a very real prospect, but she didn't let her fear of it take over.

When we live our lives with a future punishment mindset, all we see is the worst possible scenario. Instead of seeing the possibility of hope like Marie and Werner, we only see death, whether spiritual or physical. Although most of us won't face the level of risk Marie and Werner faced, we face other fears every day. And a spirit from the Enemy will always point us toward the worst-case scenario. It will whisper things like, "If you do this, you'll never survive," or "If you take this risk, you will fail." The possibility of the worst becomes greater in our minds than Jesus's love for us, and it consumes us. Jesus said the Enemy is "the father of lies," so we can be sure that anything coming out of his mouth is intended to steal, kill, and destroy (see John 8:44; 10:10).

A perfect love mindset points us toward a different scenario. It reminds our spirits that even if we face hardship, we are never alone. It tells us Jesus gives us a spirit of victory, not defeat. When I think of a perfect love mindset, I think of my love for my kids. If they have a physical or emotional need, I don't think about the cost. Even if I know the need will deplete me in a physical, mental, or emotional way, I will respond to it in love in the best way I know how.

Three Questions to Ask Yourself

Let's break these two mindsets down even further and pose some questions we can ask ourselves when faced with a decision. When we would rather stick with what we think is safe and predictable, let's uncover the root of our motivation.

The next time you feel tempted to withdraw from something you believe God prompted you to do, ask yourself the following questions.

Does this thing line up with the person I see God calling me to be? Does it line up with his purposes for you? Have you ever had one of those moments in your life when you think, "I was made for this"? Whatever it is you're doing, it makes you feel alive and energized. Even if it is physically or mentally draining, you don't feel depleted afterward. Pay attention to these signals. Many times, God reveals his purpose for us through them. Of course, his purpose for each believer is for us to share his love with those around us. But this will look different for each of us depending on our unique gifts, experiences, and abilities.

If the action or endeavor you feel prompted toward does line up, what do you have to lose? Are the things you may lose temporary, or do they carry a significance that will last? Asking these hard questions will not only reveal the root of your fear but help you to fix your focus on the One who can bring peace. Ask him to help you. Often, my worries will dissipate after a frank and honest conversation with the One who knows.

If I say no or don't take the step, will I regret my decision in the future? One of the questions I often ask my coaching clients is "What is the benefit of staying where you are?" Usually, it's comfort. We become familiar with our station in life, our abilities, and even our pain and suffering. We see a telling depiction of how this familiarity can limit us in Jesus's question to the blind man at the pool of Bethesda: "Do you want to get well?" (John 5:6).

I used to puzzle over this question and think, "Well, yeah. Duh." But then God revealed the truth to me one day. He pressed this recognition onto my spirit: "You hold on to your pain too."

Sometimes we carry junk for so long we don't realize we're carrying it. Whether it's emotional baggage, fear, or an unhealthy mindset, it's a part of us. We don't see the way it's weighing us down because it's ingrained into the fabric of our being. But God sees. He sees not only the person we are now but the person he's creating and birthing in us. He wants us to let go of everything that's hindering us and cling to him instead.

Look at one of your hands and think of the step God is asking you to take. Picture this decision being in this hand. It's the hand he's holding. Reach up, because he's pulling it ever so gently. Now picture the decision to stay where you are in the other hand. No one is pulling it, so lay it by your side. Then ask yourself, "Months or years from now, how will I feel about staying put?" Sit with that feeling for a few minutes and ask God to reveal any hidden doubts that you need to bring to him.

Do I trust God more than I trust what I can see? Friends, this is where we get to the heart of the matter. I think deep down on some level we can't quite articulate, we know when God is asking us to do something. We may try to reason our way out of it; but if we've spent time with him, we know how to recognize his promptings. So the question is this: Do we trust him? Do we trust him even when we've faced disappointment in the past and are uncertain about the future? God will never ask us to do something and then say, "Well, you're on your own now. Good luck!" He goes with us each step of the way. He is the faithful God of the beginning, middle, and end.

> God will never ask us to do something and then say, "Well, you're on your own now. Good luck!" He goes with us each step of the way.

Ask yourself each of these questions today and be honest in your responses. If your answers lead you to the realization that a future punishment mindset is dictating your life, confess this to God. He is ready and willing to help you move forward. Sometimes we just have to put our own pride aside and ask for it.

The Promise We Can Stand On

Now that we know which type of mindset we're living with, how do we move forward while staying rooted in God's truth? We are bombarded with messages each day telling us to keep our focus on ourselves, our comfort, and our safety. Knowing what drives us is one thing, but staying the course toward what God has for us is another.

For the past nine years, God has brought the words from Psalm 27 into my life. This is a popular psalm of David, so it would be easy to dismiss it as a coincidence, but each of these occurrences has been very specific and timed in a way that could only be orchestrated by God. Women I didn't know and others who had no clue what I was going through gave me verses from this psalm to meditate on. Sometimes the verses were printed out on cards, and other times they were spoken over me.

The first time this psalm came into my life in a specific, intentional way, I was at my first writer's conference. That particular year, there were over eight hundred attendees, all at different stages in their journeys. The staff prayed for days, asking God to direct them toward verses from the Bible to pick and assign to each person who came. Even without knowing these attendees, they knew God would lead.

When I arrived at my seat the first evening at the conference, I picked up the card containing my verse. It read:

For in the day of trouble
he will keep me safe in his dwelling;
he will hide me in the shelter of his sacred tent
and set me high upon a rock.

Then my head will be exalted
above the enemies who surround me;
at his sacred tent I will sacrifice with shouts of joy;
I will sing and make music to the LORD.
(Ps. 27:5–6)

God knew the doubt and apprehension I carried with me into this conference. He knew I didn't feel qualified to be there or to pursue a dream that felt too big and too risky. In the following months when I faced rejection and a sense of pointlessness, I clung to these verses and made the vow to continue to "make music to the LORD."

Years after this conference, I sat in a breast imaging waiting room. I had received a dreaded callback on an irregular screening, and my mind was reeling with possibilities. I tried to numb my mind with aimless scrolling on my phone, but my signal was terrible and I couldn't get a connection. When I looked across the room, I saw a Gideon Bible sitting on a side table.

There was a defective page cut in a way that caused it to protrude out farther than the rest of the pages. It created a sort of bookmark, and so I opened the Bible to this page. When I did, these words from Psalm 27 greeted me:

The LORD is my light and my salvation—
whom shall I fear?

> *The* LORD *is the stronghold of my life—*
> *of whom shall I be afraid?* (Ps. 27:1)

I thanked God and knew that regardless of my diagnosis, God saw me. He knew every fear I faced, and he cared enough to send the exact words I needed.

Friend, I don't know what fear is keeping you in a holding pattern today, but God does. He knows each and every detail. Turn your mind away from the swirling circumstances you face today and picture a rock. This is where he wants to bring you. High above every doubt and what-if the Enemy brings to your mind.

Close your eyes and envision yourself standing on this rock. The chaos is below you now. It's trying to reach you, but it can't because God's presence surrounds you like a cloud. The sweet music you make to the Lord deafens and blinds those who try to bring you down into the valley of fear.

Now open your eyes. This is your true self, victor. Everything else is a distraction.

DISCUSSION QUESTIONS

1. In this chapter, we talked about how our fear is usually pointing us toward something else, and how it's important to identify these "trigger points":

    - A past trauma we haven't dealt with
    - An insecurity we need to surrender to the Lord
    - A desire to see a future God hasn't yet revealed to us

    Does one of these trigger points resonate with you? What is the first step you think God wants you to take toward healing or wholeness?

2. When you picture living in a "perfect love mindset," what comes to mind? How do you think living with this type of mindset would change the way you live day-to-day life?

3. Early in the chapter, I talked about a question I often asked as a toddler when I was about to try something new: Will it hurt? As you move forward and take steps of faith with God's leading, what's a more hope-filled question you could ask yourself?

3

the tree of life called desire

Food apps can be dangerous. Especially when there's a −4 degree windchill outside. God didn't create my body for such nonsense. The drearier and colder the weather, the more I need to get out of the house, fill my stomach with something warm, and indulge myself with a treat I can only find at a local restaurant at this time of year—chicken tortilla soup. Earlier this week, I craved this little winter indulgence to warm me up, and stat. So I jumped on the app for the one place in our area that serves it and placed my order.

After I made the trip to the restaurant and the employee handed me my soup, I thanked her. Her response? "My pleasure."

The majority of those who live on the East Coast now know where I got my soup. Along with their ability to get food to your vehicle with the speed and precision of a military operation, this response is one of the staples of their service. To be honest, the restaurant just wouldn't feel the same without this phrase.

Until recently, I hadn't thought much about it. Then, when talking with a friend, Chick-fil-A somehow came up during the conversation. "I can't stand it when they say that," she said. "It makes me cringe."

I looked at her and chuckled, somewhat perplexed. I mean, seriously? I'd gotten so used to the phrase, I think I would be downright offended if they didn't say this to me after I thanked them for my food. But after giving her response some thought, I understood. The word "pleasure" had a certain connotation for her. Hearing it made her think of something sexual, something a restaurant worker shouldn't be alluding to while handing her chicken nuggets. For whatever reason, this word didn't seem appropriate in the context of fast food.

It made me wonder what other words in our language carry specific connotations with them based on a person's experience, the things they were taught, and how they use those words in day-to-day life. Take, for example, the word *desire*. When many of us hear this word, we don't typically think of our spiritual lives. We think of the flesh. According to Merriam-Webster, the definition of *desire*, when used as a noun, is a "conscious impulse toward something that promises enjoyment or satisfaction in its attainment."[1] Reading this definition, we may think of intimacy or other wants we have as humans; our walk with God isn't often the first thing that springs to mind.

While the English language has one word for desire, along with a few synonyms, Hebrew has many. When I did a word study on "desire" and its uses throughout Scripture, I found that the Old Testament has twenty-seven words translated as *desire*.[2] This includes both root words and their derivatives. One of the most frequent words used for "desire" in the Old Testament Hebrew is the word *taavah*. Want to take a guess as to the primary definition of this word? Pleasure or delight. These are the most common uses, while *desire* is another, less common one. We'll dive more into why this is important later in the chapter, but for now, I want you to note that in the Hebrew language, in which much of the Bible was written, *desire*, *delight*, and *pleasure* are often used in the same context.

Some of us don't associate desires with God at all. The reason I know this is because, for a long time, I fell into this category. I didn't tell God about them because, for one, I didn't think he was interested, and two, it didn't feel safe. For someone who craves security and certainty, confiding in an all-powerful God about my heart's deepest longings equated to putting some dollar bills in a giant claw machine and hoping for the best. Although I can't pinpoint an exact moment in time when I developed this view of God, as I looked back on my childhood, a few clues emerged.

Before we talk about these memories from the past, I want us to take a trip back. I want you, reader, to think back to your childhood. Go to a moment in time before anyone told you "You can't do that" or "That will never work." Before your view of the world was filtered by other people's opinions, whether good or bad. Perhaps you were five, and your favorite hobby was painting pictures your mom hung on the fridge. Maybe you were older, and your soccer coach always made sure you had plenty of play time during games. Envision a time when you felt safe and loved. Do you have the picture in your mind? Okay, stay there, and let's chat.

Our Hidden Keys to the Father's Heart

I never had to ask my kids what they wanted to be when they grew up. They just told me. Often, it would change more than once in a single day. Some of the occupations they shared weren't even humanly possible. But this minor inconvenience didn't deter them. In their imaginations, anything was within reach.

One day, my daughter told me she wanted to be a frog. She did so with great animation and description as I made dinner. I sautéed vegetables and smiled at her, knowing her future career as a frog would change in less than twenty-four hours. And sure enough, it did. The next day, she wanted to be a bus driver.

Although I think there are many reasons why kids name these desires for the future, a big one stands out to me: They're not afraid. My daughter doesn't have any shame in telling me she wants to be a bus driver when she's old enough to drive a car and have children of her own. And my boys, who are older, don't shy away from telling me their newest dream is to start their own YouTube channel highlighting their latest video game strategies. There is no risk in sharing these desires with me and their dad because they know we will listen, guide them with love, and encourage them.

Does this mean we never give our children words of wisdom? No. One of our jobs as parents is to train them up in the way they should go so that when they get older, they do not depart from it (Prov. 22:6). A dive into the Amplified translation of this verse reveals that it has less to do with teaching our kids right and wrong and is more about guiding them toward their natural gifts and strengths. But at the end of the day, each of our kids knows they have a safe place to talk about their goals and dreams for the future. They can divulge their latest big ideas without being laughed at or ridiculed, encouraged by the knowledge that their parents want the best for them.

> Like the mom and dad who listen to their kids talk about their latest dream, God smiles and gives his undivided attention.

I believe when God looks at us, he wants the same openness and safety. He wants us to come to him with all of it—our desires, hopes, and dreams for the future, the career goals we had when we were six but buried as an adult under a pile of disappointments and misguided comments from others, the pull we had toward art or science or engineering. And as we do, he shapes them. Like the mom and dad who listen to their kids talk about their latest dream, God smiles and gives his undivided attention. One of the most beautiful gifts we have from God once we are in Christ is his friendship. In John 15:15, Jesus tells his apostles, "I no longer call you servants, because a servant does not know his master's business. Instead, I have called you friends, for everything that I learned from my Father I have made known to you." This statement reveals a level of trust Jesus didn't offer to just anyone—only to those who had walked with him day after day, eaten with him, and prayed with him. He extends this invitation not only to his apostles but to you and me.

But somehow, amid millions of distractions and false narratives about who God is, we either forget this truth or were never aware of it to begin with. And not coming to God with the thing we want causes dissonance. The more we distance ourselves from him, the more difficult it becomes to discern his leading in our lives. And this dissonance doesn't just affect our journey with God. Over time, it affects every other area of our lives. As author Emily P. Freeman writes,

> *I cannot tell you the number of times I've had to work through layers of grief, anger, frustration, and fatigue after a life experience only to realize later the real reason for all that negativity was I had a particular desire I had not yet named. When that desire went unmet, I felt it. But I didn't know why. And so that disappointment came out in other weird ways such as irritability, insecurity, lashing out, and silent*

> *treatments. It's remarkable the lengths my subconscious will go to in order to mask my truest desire.*[3]

As Freeman points out, masking our desires doesn't lead to them going away. Instead, it leads to us projecting our hurt and disappointment onto other people. So let's ask ourselves, Why do we hide them? As we've unpacked in the previous chapters, Jesus leads his sheep. John 10 tells us he speaks to us and guides us. We know his voice. And one of the ways he speaks to us and guides us is through the desires he places within us.

Now, some of you may already be checking out mentally and saying, "Abby, I can't trust my heart or my desires. My heart is deceitful. The Bible says so" (e.g., Jer. 17:9). And yes, this is true. Our hearts can lead us down paths God never intended for us. All we must do is look back to the garden, as we discussed in Chapter One, to see how our hearts can be deceived and misled. Another verse in Scripture instructs us not to follow our hearts but to guard them (Prov. 4:23). Why? Because *everything* we do flows from it.

Here and throughout the Bible, we see our hearts equated to a spring. Our source of life. This is true not only in a literal sense but in our spiritual lives. Guarding the heart is crucial because our hearts long to be filled with something. Anything. And when we don't fill them with God's truth and his love, our desire for fulfillment will lead us to satisfy our hearts with something else. More knowledge. More power. More of anything that promises to fill the emptiness.

Yes, not all desires are indeed from God. We still live in human bodies and a world led by sin, lust, and selfishness. But in the midst of a world gone crazy, our desires are still one way God speaks to us. He plants them in us and fulfills them for his glory so that others can see his love and his power. So how do we reconcile these conflicting views of the heart? With wills and bodies often misled to pursue unhealthy habits, how can we know whether a desire is from God? Sometimes, in our uncertainty about whether a desire is from God, we decide to bury it or keep it from him. But there is a better way.

Psalm 37:4 says, "Take delight in the LORD, and he will give you the desires of your heart." Here, we see the starting point for us to view our desires being fulfilled in a healthy, whole way. When we begin with God and long for him first, our other longings will follow. But we can't long for a God we don't know. This yearning for more of him is fostered in daily habits we develop in any thriving relationship. Talking to him. Confiding in him. Seeking his guidance in the big decisions and the small ones. As we do each of these things, our thirst for him grows. And as it does, he leads us with the desires he places within us because we've shown a want for him above all else. When we look at our lives and see this type of relationship and hunger for God, we can name our desires with confidence.

But there's another facet to naming our desires that we can't overlook. And for much of my life, I didn't see it. Our perspective of who God is and how he sees us changes everything. For years, my view was distorted. Although many experiences contributed to this view, one memory stands out in my mind. I was twelve years old, sitting in the pastor's office.

The Fear We Don't Name

The chair seemed much too big for my small frame. I squirmed around and tried to get comfortable while I looked across the huge desk in front of me, covered with important papers. My heart felt as though it might pound out of my chest at any given moment.

What if I don't know the answer to a question he asks?

What was that verse we talked about in class again?

Is this what a job interview feels like?

I couldn't read the pastor's face. It wasn't unkind, but it wasn't welcoming either. I sensed he had more important things to do than sit there talking to me. After a few moments of asking me various questions about my family and making pleasantries, we dug into the stuff we were there for. The church's theology and doctrine. I did my best to recall the scriptures we'd discussed over the past six weeks, and as the discussion continued, I felt more confident. My body relaxed into the chair a bit.

Then, he asked me a question I wasn't expecting.

"So why do we do good works?"

I considered the question for a few seconds and let my heart lead me instead of my brain. I said, "To please God." My twelve-year-old brain didn't think of the word "glorify." In an instant, the chair became uncomfortable again as I studied the pastor's face and tried to predict his response. After a moment, I could tell he didn't like my answer.

"Well, we can't *please* God . . ." he said.

I backtracked and attempted to explain my answer. "No, I mean through Christ." My mind raced with a million other things I could have said.

Why did you say that?

What were you thinking?

Somehow, I redeemed my answer, but the next five minutes seemed to crawl by with no end in sight. Finally, the pastor dismissed me. I had passed the test and was deemed knowledgeable enough to be sprinkled with water the following Sunday.

I breathed a sigh of relief, but what he said stayed with me.

"You can't please God."

It wasn't until many years later that I realized how much those four words impacted me. I mean, they were just four words said in the space of seconds. But they were stated by a person I believed and respected. In my mind, this pastor was the authority on all things biblical. A part of me I couldn't quite articulate at the time thought, *Well if I can't please God, what's the point?* For years, nothing I did felt like enough. I didn't bring my desires to God. If I couldn't please him, why would he care?

Now, before we continue, I want to acknowledge the fact that yes, our works are nothing aside from Christ's finished work on the cross. Our position has nothing to do with earning his favor and everything to do with Jesus's blood, shed for you and me as a permanent payment for my sins and yours.

Okay, now that we've acknowledged those foundational truths, let's talk a bit more about what telling a twelve-year-old she can't please God does to her psyche. In short, it messes her up. Big time. Especially for a people-pleasing, will-you-please-be-my-friend girl who is in the middle of puberty. In essence, it's like saying, "You can't please your dad. So don't even try." Naming our desires indicates trust. We're not going to tell someone about a deep desire if we don't believe they will treat it with a delicate hand. In a world where we chase after certainty and guarantees, naming our desires to an unseen God feels risky. But there's another aspect to naming our desires that I didn't realize until recently: delight. When we know someone delights in us, we come to them with our desires freely. This is why my children share their dreams and desires with me and their dad without fear. They see the smiles on our faces and our eyes light up. They feel the safety of our embrace.

Naming our desires indicates trust. We're not going to tell someone about a deep desire if we don't believe they will treat it with a delicate hand.

When Psalm 37:4 tells us to delight ourselves in the Lord, it sets a precedent. Delighting ourselves in the Lord is a natural response to knowing him. We can't delight in someone we don't know and don't spend time in conversation with. But there is another aspect to this reciprocal relationship, and I think we often overlook it. We must also recognize that God *delights in us.* He rejoices over us. When we come to him with our dreams and desires, he is pleased.

My journey to see God as someone who delighted in me was a slow and sometimes painful one. When you haven't confided in God in years, it takes some major mindset shifts to bring you to a place where it feels natural to do so. One of those shifts came a few months after the birth of my first child. I remember reading one of Max Lucado's early books, and a chapter about the depths of God's love highlighted the popular verse from Zephaniah:

> *The Lord your God is with you,*
> *the Mighty Warrior who saves.*
> *He will take great delight in you;*
> *in his love he will no longer rebuke you,*
> *but will rejoice over you with singing.* (Zeph. 3:17)

These words were completely new and foreign to me. The ideas of God delighting in me and singing over me were concepts that seemed too beautiful for my brain to comprehend. But in a season of new motherhood, weariness, and isolation, I needed this Father whom Zephaniah wrote about. Instead of being the distant Father I couldn't please, he became the Dad who danced with his daughter. I grasped hold of this new idea of God and didn't let go.

Over the next several years, I immersed myself in Scripture, and God revealed his heart to me. I realized he wasn't the taskmaster I grew up believing him to be. He was pleased with me, not because I deserved his love or did anything to earn his favor, but because I was his own. The truth was as simple as it was profound. In the same way I delighted in my new son, God found joy in watching me become the woman he created.

A Tree Displaying the Lord's Splendor

As we come to God with our desires like kids whose hearts are filled with trust, he transforms us. Sick hearts enclosed by walls of fear become trees filled with fruit. Dead dreams come to life as we present them to our Father with hands open to receive whatever he has for us. Does this mean our desires will always be met in the way we want or envision? No, friend, it doesn't. We can never be certain of the outcome when we bring our desires to God. But we can be certain of this: He longs to hear from us. As we journey through this reciprocal relationship of giving and receiving, we begin to release to God what we don't see come to fruition as well.

Proverbs gives us a beautiful picture of what happens when a God-given desire is fulfilled: "Hope deferred makes the heart sick, but a desire fulfilled is a tree of life" (Prov. 13:12 ESV). At the beginning of the chapter, we talked about how in the original Hebrew language, the words *desire*, *delight*, and *pleasure* are often used in the same context. Well here, the Hebrew word for desire is that word we discussed, *taavah*. Do you know where else the word *taavah* is used? In Genesis, right before Eve eats from the Tree of Knowledge of Good and Evil.[4]

> *When the woman saw that the tree was good for food, and that it was a delight [taavah] to the eyes, and that the tree was desirable to make one wise, she took some of its fruit and ate; and she also gave some to her husband with her, and he ate.* (Gen. 3:6 NASB)

Our Desire Will Always Follow Our Delight

When we delight ourselves in the Lord, as the psalmist says, our desires will follow. But when our desires are misguided by a false sense of security, we experience death.

I find it no mistake that the writer of Proverbs uses a tree to depict what happens when this longing of our hearts is fulfilled. A tree is also what leads Eve to believe a false narrative and a desire that leads to separation from God. But throughout Scripture, trees are used as pictures of faith, resilience, and God's provision. And here, we see what a tree can do when our desires and longings are in alignment with God's best for us. We see a tree thriving because of his provision. In another passage of Scripture, children of the Lord are called "oaks of righteousness, a planting of the LORD for the display of his splendor" (Isa. 61:3).

When I envision these sturdy trees with their branches reaching toward the sun, a beautiful picture of God's character is revealed. Like the life of the tree, the desires of our hearts go through a cycle. At the beginning of the cycle, the desire is a seed. We haven't shared it with God or anyone else, and we're uncertain we ever will. But as we seek him and know him more, we see his delight in his children. That's you and me, friends. Our trust and delight in him grow, and as we invite him into each area of our lives, our relationship with him thrives. We share our desires with him, and as we do, he nurtures them and prunes them into desires that reflect his heart. Then, in his timing and according to his will, we see the desire become a reality, a beautiful tree on display for others to see and witness God's love.

Friend, I don't know what desires and dreams you've kept buried, hidden from God out of fear of what may happen if you share them. Perhaps you did share them with him but are in a long season of waiting. You're beginning to doubt you will ever see the tree described in Proverbs and believe the seed you left in God's care is dead and buried. Can I share something with you? We serve a God who loves to resurrect dead things. And often it's in this process of resurrection that he creates something even more magnificent.

As you come to God with the desires of your heart, here is a daily three-part prayer to guide you. Feel free to adapt this prayer to your individual situation and needs. It is meant to serve as a blueprint.

1. **Acknowledge our need.**
   God, I need you. I know that apart from your Spirit, I am misled by the temporary things of this world. Align my heart with yours and help me to lay aside anything that will hinder my relationship with you. You are my heart's first and foremost desire, and I want to honor and glorify your name.
2. **Express gratitude for God's provision.**
   Thank you for knowing what I need and desire before I even ask. Thank you for the ability to come to you openly with my heart's desires, and for your tender attention to each one. I know that no request is too big or too small for you, and you delight in each detail of my life (Ps. 37:23–25 NLT).
3. **Present our desires to him.**
   God, this is my heart's desire. (Tell him what it is.) You know the road ahead of me and each person with whom my life will intersect in the days to come. If this desire is from you, God, may it be so. I pray for it to become a beautiful tree that displays your provision

> and your love, so others may see it and praise your name. And God, if this desire is not from you, please make this truth known to me. Guide me with your Word and help me to release anything that will not lead to your perfect peace.
>
> In Jesus's name, amen.

When I pray this prayer, it is a release. No matter the outcome, I know my desires are in the hands of the One who knows me best. He sees what's beneath my request and knows whether it leads me further in becoming the woman he created me to be. As the tension in my body loosens and I let go of my need for certainty, my soul finds the rest it needs.

DISCUSSION QUESTIONS

1. In this chapter, we talked about how God often speaks to us through our desires. Do you bring your desires to God? Why or why not?

2. Kids will often name their desires without fear. Why do you think it is easier for kids to name their desires? Do you remember any specific desires you had as a kid that you later abandoned?

3. Our view of who God is will always affect whether or not we trust him with our desires. As you consider your view of him, do you think it's filtered by love or an unhealthy fear?

4

you don't need someone else to tell you what God is saying

My eyes followed the lead pastor as he exited the stage and headed toward the back of the sanctuary. Already, people were following him and talking to him, no doubt asking questions about the message. In a congregation with numbers reaching into the thousands, he's a popular guy on Sunday mornings. But I was determined.

"I'm going to go get Jaden."

I nodded to my husband as he turned toward the nursery, but my attention was still on Pastor Rick. After grabbing my coat, I walked toward him, rehearsing words. For weeks, a question had been at the forefront of my mind, and I was confident he'd know the answer. Congregants continued to follow and converse with him, so when I reached him, I stood there feeling rather awkward. He glanced my way at one point, his eyes saying,

"Do you have a question?" After a man gushed compliments and left, I saw my opening.

"Do you believe once a person is saved, they're always saved?" I blurted out. Pastor Rick got a furrow in his brow like I'd just hit him in the stomach. But I continued. I told him about a loved one who was making poor choices and causing our family a lot of heartache. Without going into much detail, I told him I was worried. My eyes pleaded for an affirmation, expecting him to give me a yes or no answer along with a list of verses to support his response.

"I don't know," he said.

I looked at him and opened my mouth, shifting from one leg to the other.

He doesn't know? How can he not know? Didn't he go to seminary and spend countless hours studying these age-old questions?

"Trying to answer that question is like hitting my head up against a brick wall," he continued, "but I'd like to think once we enter into that relationship, it is secure." He added little to further explain his response but told me the church would keep our family in prayer. Then he diverted his eyes toward my husband, who was walking up with our firstborn. Jaden was all smiles. A hand-crocheted hat, a gift from a friend, sat on his head.

"Nice hat," the pastor said, finished with our conversation.

We said a few pleasantries to the others who were now standing there, and then our family headed toward the door. I continued to replay the conversation in my head, still in disbelief over the pastor's response.

At this point in my faith journey, I was experiencing a period of extreme growth and resurgence. My Bible was a gold mine filled with scripture I'd never explored, and I couldn't get enough. But with this newfound thirst came questions. On numerous occasions, I encountered verses that seemed to contradict each other or read stories that left me wondering, *What does this mean?* My conversation with the pastor was a result not only of my concern for my loved one but also of one of these moments of uncertainty and questions. But instead of receiving the certainty I longed for, I continued to question what the future held.

The following Sunday, we sat in our small group and chatted with the other attendees before diving into the week's lesson. I brought up my conversation with the pastor and two men in the class looked at me in disbelief.

"He said he didn't know?!" they exclaimed in unison.

I nodded, elaborating on a few details but not feeling the need to defend his response. For some reason I didn't yet understand, each time I spoke about it, I felt more at peace with his answer. But Tom, one of the class attendees, wasn't having it. He offered me several book recommendations to answer my question, all of which would give a resounding *yes*. I thanked him for his input but declined.

It's been fifteen years since the conversation with my pastor. Since then, my husband and I have moved cross-country, had two more kids, and walked through countless struggles, joys, and questions. The more I continue to grow and know God, the more I respect Pastor Rick's answer. He didn't know. And he was brave enough to not conjure up an answer or say what I wanted to hear. He was honest. In a world where spiritual leaders are expected to serve up answers like hot coffee on Sunday morning, his response took courage.

Brave Enough to Do the Searching

Most of us are searching for an answer to a life-altering question. And if we aren't right now, we will be. These questions often keep us awake at night and give us constant, low-grade anxiety. When will the sickness end? When will my family member stop running? How will I know whether to take the job? These questions are important to the trajectory of our lives and the lives of others. In our search, we might pray, seek God's guidance, and wait for his leading. But often, we go to others first. Without even asking for God's wisdom, we look to our pastor, friend, or family member for the answer to our burning question. Why? Because we want certainty; and on some level, we think a flesh and blood person who is standing in front of us can give us more of it than the God of the universe. On the surface, there isn't anything wrong with asking others for guidance and wisdom, but when it becomes a habit, we miss opportunities for our faith to mature and develop.

When Jesus said, "My sheep hear my voice," he didn't qualify it by saying, "My sheep need an interpreter." He didn't say, "Some sheep hear my voice, but others need a special sheep to tell them what I'm saying to them." Now, this does not mean to go off in a pasture by ourselves, away from the other sheep. Sheep are not solitary animals. It also doesn't mean we don't have spiritual leaders and mentors to offer wisdom and guidance. But here's the thing, when we rely solely on someone else to digest the words of God for us, we have a problem. Our growth will be limited, and we will restrict our confidence in our ability to discern God's voice for ourselves. Not only that, but we are missing out on one of the greatest gifts Jesus gave us when he ascended into heaven: access to our Helper, the Holy Spirit, who speaks to each one of us in a unique way.

More often than I care to admit, I miss out on the lavishness of this gift because I'm willing to settle for scraps. Instead of taking the time to go to God and lay out every burden before him, I settle for an inspirational meme on Instagram. When my soul needs the guidance and nourishment only he can provide, I seek others' opinions before seeking the living God.

Friends, let me reiterate that there's nothing wrong with seeking wise counsel. God tells us to be in community with other believers and to not forsake this practice. But here's what we need to remember. We can't let the counsel of others replace the counsel of the living God. It's not worth it. His presence and his words are too great of a treasure to throw away because we decide to settle for the instantaneous satisfaction of scrolling and text messages. We need his truth, straight from the heart of the One who sacrificed everything so that we could receive it without restriction.

> We can't let the counsel of others replace the counsel of the living God.

In our desire for certainty and answers, we tell ourselves something like this: *I can't be sure of what God is saying to me. I haven't read my Bible enough.* Or we might think, *This person really seems to have her prayer life more together than I do. I should ask her to pray for me instead of praying for myself.* I know these mindsets and these internal monologues because I've had them myself. I've reasoned my way out of trusting a word God gave me because I didn't think I was spiritual enough, holy enough, or well-versed in Scripture enough.

Because we serve a gracious God, he sends us reminders. Last week, he sent me one in an unexpected book of the Bible—Exodus. At the beginning of the year, I committed to reading through the entire Bible in a year, and this week's reading detailed the building of the tabernacle. Friend, I must admit this section of text was difficult for me to get through. Chapter after chapter contain God's specific instructions for the materials to be used, the dimensions, what the priests were to wear, and how to consecrate themselves before entering. The penalty for breaking many of these rules was death. In the Western world, we are far removed from ancient Israelite culture, and these strict guidelines may be difficult to understand. But when we view them in the context of a holy God doing everything in his power to maintain communion with his people, these instructions take on a new meaning. This tabernacle was the place where God's presence would dwell and priests would make atonement for their community's sins. And for this to happen, the structure had to be set apart as holy.

Because the Israelites followed each guideline from the Lord exactly as it was given, his presence dwelled with them throughout their journey. His habitation of the tent was not assumed; it was visible in a clear, tangible way. Their community didn't have to speculate about whether God was with them and guiding them. His glory emanated from the place they built, and he honored their obedience.

> *The Israelites set out whenever the cloud was taken up from the tabernacle throughout all the stages of their journey. If the cloud was not taken up, they did not set out until the day it was taken up. For the cloud of the* LORD *was over the tabernacle by day, and there was a fire inside the cloud by night, visible to the entire house of Israel throughout all the stages of their journey.* (Exod. 40:36–38 CSB)

As I read chapter after chapter of extensive, detailed instructions, the gift you and I possess came alive in a way I hadn't known before. In the past, I understood the death and the blood of Jesus. In my own limited way, I saw the sacrifice. But now I understand the burden he lifted from his people through this perfect sacrifice, the one you and I could never offer. The fact that the temple wasn't limited to the place the priests entered after washing themselves, sprinkling themselves with blood, and offering the sacrifice was a gift I had taken for granted. In my removed, privileged state, it had become commonplace. But now I saw it for the stunning grace it is. His temple is my body. It's yours. The holy place now resides in each one of us who have said yes to him.

Paul reminds us of the high price God paid for us to receive this unlimited access to his Spirit, saying, "Do you not know that your bodies are temples of the Holy Spirit, who is in you, whom you have received from God? You are not your own; you were bought at a price" (1 Cor. 6:19–20). So, what does this mean for us today? In the context of our day-to-day lives, how does this affect our actions, conversations, and attitudes? When we understand the unsurpassed value of this gift, it affects everything. Nothing in our lives is off-limits. Instead of needing a high priest to enter the holy place and intercede on our behalf, we can talk to God each moment of our day. We can come to him with the questions and the hang-ups. We can ask for his wisdom in areas of our lives where we feel stuck and discouraged.

When I felt stuck over the question I asked my pastor, he didn't offer me a resolution. Although his lack of an answer frustrated me at the moment, I later realized his honesty was an invitation. His "I don't know" caused me to seek the One who did. And as I came to God with a thirst to know *him* more than to know an answer, he guided my heart toward truth. He gave me the assurance and the peace I longed for, and this peace wouldn't have come through easy responses or hurried resolution. It wouldn't have come without the grit wrought through waiting. My pastor's uncertainty ended up being a hidden gift, one that led me straight to the heart of the One who holds all certainty in his hands.

> We must accept the paradox that while we tend to want either/or explanations and paths, we serve a God who loves to say "and."

Seeking God ourselves takes courage. We must put aside our need to always "get it right" and our tendencies toward quick black-and-white responses. We must accept the paradox that while we tend to want either/or explanations and paths, we serve a God who loves to say "and." He wants us to seek him *and* trust the power of the Spirit he's given us. He wants us to set the boundary with the difficult family member *and* love her through it.

Sometimes when we seek God's direction, he leads us back to ourselves. Not because he wants to frustrate us or promote self-sufficiency, but because he wants us to grow. He wants us to know his voice, follow it, and make faith-building decisions with confidence.

As I've spent the past couple of decades walking with him and learning to recognize his nudges, I've noticed patterns. His voice doesn't change like the wind but is steady and consistent. Its attributes are recognizable. When something in our spirit feels jarred and off, we need to pay attention. In the way we know a lifelong friend we regularly meet for coffee, we will sense discrepancies when the voice of the Father we know is different from the one who claims to speak for him.

When the Voice You Hear Is an Imposter

Yesterday evening, I received a text message from someone who claimed to be my boss. Not only did this person know my name, but he or she also knew the first and last name of the CEO of my company. The message I received asked me to confirm who I was. This should have been my first red flag, but I thought perhaps he had multiple phone numbers for me. So, I obliged. Then he said he was in a meeting with stakeholders of our company, and he needed me to perform an urgent task. At this point, the bells alerting "scammer" went off.

If you've spent any time on social media or have a cell phone, you know scammers are becoming more and more clever. They will use any means possible to lure you into their ploys and then use the pieces of your identity you've given them to take what they want. This person texting me was no different.

So, as with any suspected scammer, I asked myself some key questions. Was this method of contact normal for the person they claimed to be? In this case, the answer was no. My boss never texted me. He used a project management app or sometimes email. This was my first red flag. Next, I asked myself if the message was in the familiar voice of this person. While it was similar, I had never heard my boss use the word *urgent*. It was also rare for him to ask me to perform this type of task, and even rarer for him to ask me to do so at 8:15 p.m.

I put all these pieces together and concluded that more than likely, this was not my boss texting me. To make sure, I reached out to him via the aforementioned app. Within thirty minutes, he responded and said I was indeed dealing with a scammer. This imposter had reached out not only to me but to several other people I worked with. Although it's unclear how the scammer obtained our information, one thing was clear: They needed to be blocked and reported.

As I thought about this scenario and the rise of identity theft in our nation, it made me think of the ways people misrepresent God as well. Sometimes the misrepresentation is intentional, like the person who texted me. Their intentions are selfish and there is no amount of truth in their claims. Other times, the person is misinformed. They do not have malicious intent, but they haven't spent enough time with God or in his Word to know any better. Their words reflect the culture around them, and they think they are being helpful.

In either case, it's important for us to ask ourselves questions. God gave us gut instinct for a reason. When something feels off and makes us furrow our eyebrows, it's a good indicator of something being untrue, unsafe, or both. This does not mean the Spirit of God or his voice will always make us comfortable. On the contrary, sometimes he asks us to do things that make us quite uncomfortable and feel out of our element. But the voice of the Spirit is not inconsistent. He will never speak to us in a way that is contrary to his nature.

As we discussed in Chapter Two, Jesus's sheep have spent enough time with him to know when an impostor has entered the pasture. His sheep will not follow the voice of a stranger. He even goes a step further and says his sheep will run from a stranger.

> *They will never follow a stranger; in fact, they will run away from him because they do not recognize a stranger's voice.* (John 10:5)

We know from reading the Gospels that Jesus never said anything he didn't mean. And even though he's using word pictures here to convey his point, his meaning is clear. So how do we know whether the voice we hear is a stranger's?

Here are three characteristics of the voice of God that will help us know if we're being misled.

It's consistent and steady. When we see the Lord speaking in the Old Testament, it is almost always to bring order to chaos and light to the darkness. His voice does not bring confusion, and it is consistent with the character he's established with his people. And when God changes his mind about something in Scripture, it's usually about withholding judgment. We see this in Exodus when Moses convinces him not to destroy the entire nation of Israel after they worshiped a golden calf in place of their God (Exod. 32:14).

However, when it comes to God's ultimate will for our lives, it remains unchanging. We're to love him and honor him. We're to be an extension of his love to those we do life with and draw others to Christ through our words and actions. If we hear a voice that contradicts this command from God or promotes a self-serving, prideful nature, we are not hearing the voice of God. We need to be on our guard and proceed with discernment. We can go to him in prayer, asking him to guide us and give us insight. If we ask him for wisdom, he will give it to us freely. All we must do is ask.

It brings peace amid uncertainty. Even when I'm facing stressful circumstances, God's Word and his voice bring me peace. This peace enveloped me when I faced an unknown health diagnosis, when my son was in the hospital, and when both of my parents suffered strokes less than five months apart. It covered me when my husband and I navigated a new town and started a family without the familiarity of the home where I grew up. As Paul stated in Philippians, this peace transcends all understanding (Phil. 4:7).

If I don't feel peace, it's usually a sign that I am following a voice other than God's. My husband's work colleague declared "What are you going to do?!" after hearing of our move with a son on the way; but when I ruminated on those words, I realized it wasn't the voice of God speaking. When I questioned whether or not I had what it took to be a mother, it wasn't the voice of God either.

Sometimes misrepresentations of God's voice come from misinformed people, and other times they come from the Enemy. But either way, they often invoke shame, fear, and anxiety of the unknown. When I encounter these types of situations, one way I recenter myself in God's truth is through breath prayers. This is a type of prayer I learned a few years ago, and it takes simple, short prayers and combines them with breathing techniques to calm our hearts and minds. The neurological benefits of these prayers are manifold, showing they can rewire our brains.

In her book, *Breath as Prayer*, Jennifer Tucker explains the concept further:

> *Breath prayers combine two powerful tools that can help calm anxiety: the science of deep breathing and prayers of meditation on God's Word. . . .*
>
> *[Breath prayers] are:*
>
> - *Short, mostly one-sentence prayers*
> - *Rooted in Scripture*
> - *Aligned with the rhythm of the breath: first half is prayed while inhaling, second half is prayed while exhaling*
> - *Repeated several times for the purpose of meditating on God's word. . . .*
>
> *. . . as you practice breath prayers, you actually begin to change the neural networks in your brain. In science, they call this neuroplasticity: your brain is a dynamic organ that can literally be changed and reshaped as you learn and grow and experience new things. I like to think of it as a remarkable example of how you are literally being "transformed by the renewing of your mind"* (Romans 12:2).[1]

Through this simple practice, the voice of God becomes louder than other voices clamoring for my attention. His peace once again rules my heart, and I can move forward in confidence rather than fear.

It propels us forward. God desires for us to grow. He wants us to move from glory to glory as we become more and more like the One who created us in his image. Paul describes this movement in 2 Corinthians and reminds us of the closeness we now have with the One who spoke to Moses face to face. While Moses had to veil his face after speaking to the Lord, we have the amazing privilege of reflecting his brilliance with unveiled faces.

> *We all, with unveiled faces, are looking as in a mirror at the glory of the Lord and are being transformed into the same image from glory to glory; this is from the Lord who is the Spirit.* (2 Cor. 3:18 CSB)

Often, this movement from glory to glory means getting uncomfortable. It might mean talking to the person no one else wants to talk to or sending someone a message when you have no clue how they'll receive it. It also might involve learning a new skill or embarking on a journey that's scary and unfamiliar to us. This doesn't necessarily refer to a change in geographical location but a change in our state of mind. Growing in step with the Spirit does not mean feeding our restlessness but feeding our souls.

Sometimes, our growth is internal and may not be apparent to anyone. Other times, it is obvious, and others will be drawn to the light emanating from us. But regardless of whether the journey from glory to glory is inward or outward, it is valuable and meaningful. When we hear a voice telling us to remain stagnant or dwell in the past, we need to be mindful and alert.

While revisiting the past is sometimes necessary for healing, God doesn't want us to remain stuck there. He wants us to move toward him and with him, and he is not a stationary God.

When we hear a voice telling us to remain stagnant or dwell in the past, we need to be mindful and alert.

Abiding in the One Who Knows

Followers of Jesus who remain stationary are often afraid to ask questions. They don't want to offend the person who is in charge or offend God. They don't want to disrupt the status quo or make anyone uncomfortable. I know these mindsets because I've been one of these people. I've been the person who stays quiet in her seat, even when my insides feel like they're burning, yelling "Speak up!" While God is stretching me in this area, it is an ongoing battle.

When I went to my lead pastor with my question over a decade ago, I didn't receive the answer I wanted. But my honesty in my questions became the catalyst for my growth. His "I don't know" didn't stop me from searching for truth. It simply propelled me toward the Author of truth. And here's what I realized: Abiding in Christ means being honest with him. It means coming to him in every struggle, even when it feels scary. Even when we're afraid the truth will be harder to face than a lie.

As we do this, our desire for truth and certainty will be met by the One who speaks tomorrows into existence. But our security won't be in knowing the future or what tomorrow will bring. Our security will be in knowing him. It will be in the realization that our Author and Finisher sees every doubt, struggle, and question, and gives us what we need for today. Wisdom for today. Guidance to our next step for today. Truth for today. And in each of these things, he gives us hope for tomorrow.

DISCUSSION QUESTIONS

1. Do you doubt your ability to discern God's voice? Why or why not?

2. In this chapter, we talked about three key characteristics of God's voice: It's consistent and steady, it brings peace amid uncertainty, and it propels us forward. What characteristics would you add to this list? What would you say signals that a voice is not from God?

3. Do you tend to go to others for guidance before going to God? How do you think this affects your ability to discern his leading?

PART TWO

HE HELPS YOU TO MAKE GOOD DECISIONS

"They will come in and go out, and find pasture."

John 10:9

5

God's will for you is not a multiple-choice test

I tried not to panic. I looked around me and attempted to get my bearings, but all the islands appeared the same. Other jet skis passed by as I slowed down and released my hand from the throttle, trying to remember where to turn.

Aside from my complete loss of direction, it was the perfect lake day. The South Carolina sun reflected off soft waves, but it wasn't blazing hot like it typically is that time of year. With a week until school started, this quick trip to see my parents was part of our family's decision to soak up the last days of loose schedules. A little bit of cloud cover provided relief, giving the illusion of rain on the way. But as a former South Carolinian of twenty-eight years, I knew it was just humidity.

After idling for a moment, I headed left and accelerated. We glided across the water for a short time before I heard my son's voice behind me.

"Where are you going? You need to go right."

Right then I realized my fifteen-year-old had a better sense of direction than I did.

"Okay!" I yelled back to him. I corrected my course and wondered why I hadn't asked for his help sooner. After that, every time we needed to alter direction, I heard his voice behind me, directing me. A few minutes later, we entered the no-wake zone and I saw the dock up ahead. I breathed a sigh of relief as we got closer, and I noticed my dad standing there, waiting. Even though we weren't gone for more than thirty minutes, he was already worried.

"Thanks for your help, bud." I turned and looked at my son as we docked.

"Sure," he said, an amused smirk on his face.

We hopped off the watercraft and waded toward the shoreline. In my mind, I decided I would never go out on the lake alone. This incident was enough to make me see my need for a navigator, and since my dad's jet ski is not equipped with a GPS, the boys in my life will do.

As I think back on this experience with my son, it reminds me of several seasons of life when I felt like that lost jet skier on the lake, wondering which way to turn. I wanted nothing more than for God to give me a clear, black-and-white sign telling me I was headed in the right direction. And if the sign had flashing lights, bells, and whistles on it, even better. But more often than not, God is more like the soft voice of my son behind me, saying, "Go this way." His guidance is more of a nudge than a push, and it's more like a calm counselor than a shouting conductor. Sometimes we wish for the shouting conductor, though, don't we?

For much of my early life, I perceived God's will as something illusive and difficult to discern. I envisioned a stern headmaster standing just outside my line of sight, waiting for me to mess up, make the wrong decision, or mishear him. Whether or not this would happen wasn't a question. It was inevitable. In essence, it felt safer to do nothing. I didn't have to worry about making the headmaster angry, because if I didn't move, he would have nothing to hold against me. As I learned more about God through his Word, through prayer, and an ongoing, living relationship with him, I discovered he is for me. And when someone is for you, they want you to flourish.

God wants you to thrive and grow, taking steps forward. Even when you fall, brush yourself off and get back up again. He's not waiting for you to trip and falter. He's watching you like the dad in the front row of the dance recital, face beaming at the daughter he loves.

> As I learned more about God through his Word, through prayer, and an ongoing, living relationship with him, I discovered he is for me. And when someone is for you, they want you to flourish.

Even though my heart knows this, every now and then I still get stuck in the state of paralysis. A major decision looms and I worry about taking the wrong path. I long to be in the will of God and think there is one exact choice he wants me to make. If I don't pick this route, my life will turn into complete turmoil. So instead of trusting the Spirit to guide me and say, "This is the way; walk in it," I freeze. My anxiety over making the wrong decision becomes louder than the voice of God, who says, "You are free."

Several years ago, Randy and Tessa—a missionary couple our church supports—spoke to the congregation during Missions Week. They discussed these big life choices we often get stuck on and talked about discerning the will of God. Their work in East Africa and their journey to become missionaries were filled with twists and turns, lots of prayer, and travel to places they once vowed they would never go. They talked onstage with our pastor, and they took questions from the congregation at the end. In the last few minutes, the conversation turned toward this question many of us were asking: How do we know we're making choices in alignment with God's will? Pastor Tim said, "I've gotten hung up at times in my life, and I know others have too, where it's like, 'Well I want to do it, but I just don't know if it's what God wants me to do.'"

Then Randy, who spends much of his time in Africa training pastors and writing teaching curricula, said something I'll never forget:

> I actually talk about this a lot because it's an issue that comes up. There's this idea God's will is something like a, b, c, d, e, f, g. And I have this host of decisions that are in front of me, and if God doesn't give me the right direction, I'm going to make a bad decision and end up going from *a* to *f* or something, the wrong way, right? But that's not what Scripture teaches. We have a whole book of Proverbs, and the whole thing is designed to help you make decisions, and decisions at the pace of life. At any given time, we all have a myriad of decisions to make, and God gives us permission to say, "Okay Lord, I need to make a choice here. Please help me to make the right one." And he does. You might go this way and you might go this way, but they're both good choices.[1]

After Randy said this, I could almost hear the collective sigh of relief around me. How many of us have spent days and months waiting for God to show us an exact path, thinking there was only one correct way to go? How many times have we stalled because we envisioned his will being like this multiple-choice test Randy described, and we anguished over picking the wrong answer? I can't count the number of times I have done this, and I wonder how much of my life I've wasted in this type of mindset. Time when instead of worrying about God's will and purpose in my life, I could be living it. But as I listened to Randy and Tessa tell their story, not once did I question whether they were doing the Lord's work. Not once did I think they took a wrong turn somewhere and missed the will of God. Their lives shined as a living testimony, showing each one of us that God's Spirit is alive, and he guides each of us who seek him.

God gave us the ability to make decisions so we would exercise this ability. Yes, some choices dishonor God. We need only to look at Scripture to see this. But if you feel the nudge to do something that lines up with his Word, and it brings him glory, do it. Don't hesitate. Randy and Tessa's lives are a beautiful example of the impact we can have when we act in faith.

Like my son riding with me on the back of the jet ski, God tells us, "Whether you turn to the right or to the left, your ears will hear a voice behind you saying, 'This is the way; walk in it'" (Isa. 30:21). I'd heard that verse dozens of times, but what struck me recently as I read it was that it doesn't say, "Only if you turn to the right" or "only to the left." It tells us that in *each* path, they would hear the voice of God behind them leading the way. This promise came after Israel had messed up and disobeyed God countless times, so I find it reassuring to see God, in his grace and mercy, continue to lead them despite their flaws.

Sometimes, the reason we don't respond to the voice behind us is because we want it to be louder or more obvious. In the conversation with our pastor, Randy emphasized that he was not a "Damascus Road" type of person. In other words, he didn't have those lightning bolt moments with God like Paul on the road to Damascus, where God's path was as obvious as his command, "Now get up and go into the city, and you will be told what you must do" (Acts 9:6). Randy's journey to become a full-time missionary looked more like a series of small decisions taking place over many years. In each of these instances, he asked questions like, "What resources has God given me? What experiences do I have that could help me serve him? Does this path line up with what God commanded us to do in Scripture?" Asking these types of questions helped Randy and Tessa move forward with confidence instead of doubting and stalling.

Did this mean the road ahead of them was certain? No, it didn't. The future held many unknowns and questions they didn't yet have answers to. They were parents to young children whose lives were enmeshed with the choices they made. Would they thrive in an unstable country with political unrest? Would they get the education they needed to pursue the livelihoods they desired when they came of age? But the uncertainties of the future didn't keep them from trusting God in the present. God used circumstances in their daily lives and people they met along the way to confirm their direction and say, "Yes, keep going."

Randy and Tessa's journey is a perfect picture of the next truth we will explore from John 10. When I think about their testimony and journey, I envision an abundant green pasture with a stream flowing along the perimeter. I see a Shepherd leading the sheep with his gentle, steady voice, knowing they are his.

The Abundant Pasture of Life with Jesus

Jesus longs to give us an abundant life, not an anxious one filled with inertia. To illustrate this, we will spend the next few chapters exploring the second truth he speaks to the Pharisees in

John 10: "I am the gate; whoever enters through me will be saved. They will come in and go out, and find pasture" (John 10:9).

The pasture Jesus speaks of here is one he gives to his followers. He leads his sheep there, and they are free to move about it without fear, doubt, or mistrust.

Adam Clarke's commentary on the Bible expands on this concept of "go in and come out," saying,

> *This phrase, in the style of the Hebrews, points out all the actions of a man's life, and the liberty he has of acting, or not acting. A good shepherd conducts his flock to the fields where good pasturage is to be found; watches over them while there, and brings them back again and secures them in the fold. So he that is taught and called of God feeds the flock of Christ with those truths of his word of grace which nourish them unto eternal life; and God blesses together both the shepherd and the sheep, so that going out and coming in they find pasture: every occurrence is made useful to them; and all things work together for their good.*[2]

Did you catch the reference to a passage most of us are familiar with in the last sentence? The commentary refers to Romans 8:28, "And we know that in all things God works for the good of those who love him, who have been called according to his purpose." I find this interesting because most of us hear this verse used when people go through trials and hardship. Whether comforting or not, it's used to reassure those who are grieving a loss or dealing with an unexpected tragedy. But here, we see it used to address another simple truth: In this life, we will falter and mess up. Our place in the pasture led by the Good Shepherd does not make us perfect, at least in this life. We still live in human bodies and a world filled with other fallen people led by selfish desires. The question is not if we will falter but when. And when we do, God can use even those situations for our good and his glory. His grace envelops all of it.

As God's sheep, we have the freedom to move about this pasture Jesus describes. We are free because this is Jesus's pasture, and he led us here. It is filled with good food and a life rich with meaning and purpose. But to enjoy this rich life as his sheep, we must move. Sheep do not stay in one place. Here are two ways we come, go, and find pasture.

We feast on the Word of God and believe what it says. When we feast on something, it is our life source. We don't stand at the pantry and graze like my kids do, eating Goldfish and Twinkies every five minutes. We dig in and take notice of the intricacies and details. We learn the context of passages and how they apply to us.

Over the past several years of reading the Bible, I noticed something: Desire follows discipline, not the other way around. I don't always want to open my Bible, but I choose to. I set aside time each day to read, even when I encounter difficult passages I don't understand. And as I do this, my desire grows. I want more. My thirst for God's Word is fed by my conscious decision to feast on it despite my emotions. But reading the Bible is only the beginning. I must believe what it says to enjoy this rich, abundant pasture Jesus speaks of.

Sometimes I come across a passage of Scripture describing the early disciples' courageous acts of faith and miracles and think, "Well, that must have been nice for them." They saw Jesus in the flesh and heard him speak. They touched him and ate with him. And yet, I have access to a Helper Jesus described as being even better than his physical presence: the Holy Spirit.

In John 14, Jesus refers to the Holy Spirit as a Counselor or Advocate. He guides us, provides comfort in our time of need, and intercedes on our behalf. He is the same Helper who led the first disciples and gave them the power to perform miracles even greater than those Jesus performed during his ministry. But often, I forget his power. I stress over a situation instead of going to my Helper, my Friend, the One who is always there.

I don't want to miss out on this gift, the unlimited access to my Helper, because I decided to graze instead of feast. I want to trust that he guides me, even when I feel inadequate. I want to believe he intercedes for me, even when I don't have the words. His power is in me, and his mercy is for me. And so I cry out, "I do believe; help my unbelief!" (Mark 9:24 CSB).

We make decisions in faith, knowing our Shepherd is with us. It's important to note a repeated fact Jesus makes clear in John 10: His sheep came through the only true gate, and this gate leads to eternal life (John 10:7, 28). They didn't come in another way, led by a thief or a robber. Jesus himself is the gate, and he watches over them. He lays his life down for them and keeps them safe.

Why is this aspect of the passage crucial? Because as Jesus's followers, we still fear being misled. All we have to do is jump on social media to hear about the latest pastor or ministry leader who has taken a path contrary to what God intended. And many times, due to a lack of discernment, others follow. This passage in John doesn't say the pasture will be free of false shepherds, or as Jesus calls them, "hired hands." The key difference between the hired hand and the true Shepherd is this: one runs when trouble comes, and the other one does not. Jesus stays. His commitment to his sheep is unwavering. Even when we scatter in the chaos left by the hired hand, he comes after us. He continues to guide us with his steady, gentle voice. He's not going anywhere.

> Jesus doesn't warn us about our limitations to prompt us to do nothing. He warns us to propel us toward the One who leads us forward.

As we feast on God's Word and believe what it says, we learn to discern his Spirit's prompts and nudges. As Jesus says in John 15, we abide in him, knowing that apart from him we can do nothing. But knowing the source of our power, sustenance, and safe pasture is the beginning, not the end. Jesus doesn't warn us about our limitations to prompt us to do nothing. He warns us to propel us toward the One who leads us forward. By making decisions and moving about in his pasture, we create an abundant life in the land God gave us to enjoy. I picture the Israelites when they were about to enter the promised land. As Moses prepared to enter, he recalled their journey and the words God gave him to speak.

> *The LORD our God said to us at Horeb, "You have stayed long enough at this mountain. Break camp and advance into the hill country . . . . See, I have given you this land. Go in and take possession of the land the LORD swore he would give to your fathers—to Abraham, Isaac, and Jacob—and to their descendants after them."* (Deut. 1:6–8)

If you're familiar with this story, you know the Israelites did not take possession of the land the first time the Lord instructed them to do so. Because of their lack of faith, an entire generation died in the wilderness, leaving only their sons and daughters to walk into the fullness of God's promise. We will dive more into this disaster in judgment in a future chapter, but for now, it will suffice to say this—the Israelites forgot who God was.

I don't want to waste my life wandering like the Israelites because I'm afraid to move in the pasture Jesus gave his life for me to enjoy. I want to act in his love, knowing he will guide me and give me everything I need to take steps with wisdom. As I do this, I become a witness to others.

Not only do our decision-making and movement help us to hear God with more confidence, but they lead others into the pasture as well. When others see us responding to God's voice and using the gifts he gives us, they will be drawn toward us. By moving in the freedom God gives us, we demonstrate to others outside the pasture that God's will does not restrict our growth but enables us to thrive and live life "to the full" (John 10:10).

Come Off the Mountain of Doubt and Take the Land

When we approach his will like a multiple-choice test, we forget one of the most faith-building gifts he gives us: the ability to make good decisions. I think one of the reasons why we view God's will in this way is because we live in a culture where extremes abound. You're either type A or B. You're conservative or liberal. Introverted or extroverted. Sure, we can say we're middle of the road, independent, or an ambivert, but if we do this, we're usually called indecisive. Our vote doesn't count, and we're led to believe we're one of those who doesn't quite fit in.

When we assume there's one correct choice, life feels safe. Somehow, we believe picking the right answer will provide insurance for the road ahead. We think choosing one way over another will guarantee the protection of our careers and homes from the unseen pitfalls that lay ahead. But friends, Jesus is our only guarantee. He is the security we long for, and he is the constant presence we need when we encounter the unexpected. Trouble will come for us, but he will never leave.

A few weeks ago, my kids watched the movie *Apollo 13* for the first time. The 1995 movie starring Tom Hanks is based on the true story of the Apollo 13 space mission, which would have been the United States' third landing on the moon. Due to an explosion that damaged the craft's oxygen tank, the mission to land on the moon had to be aborted, and several modifications were made to the ship to preserve the lives of the astronauts on board. Their oxygen and potable water were depleted, and the crew had to live in freezing conditions for the last few days of their flight. Despite a scary reentry into the earth's atmosphere, lasting over a minute longer than usual, the crew landed in the South Pacific Ocean while tens of millions of viewers watched on live television.

As I watched this movie for the first time in almost two decades, several factors about the crew's odds of survival caught my attention. In short, the astronauts' safe landing was nothing short of a miracle. But one aspect of their trip home made my jaw drop. It takes place midway through the movie, when several teams on the ground are working night and day to conserve the energy and resources the team has left, knowing it will take massive amounts of energy to reenter the earth's atmosphere. This point in the return flight is a major concern because the astronauts have to navigate the reentry without many of the tools they had available to them before the explosion.

If they were landing on the moon, precision wouldn't be as much of an issue. But entering the earth's atmosphere? To be successful, they had to hit a target as thin as a piece of paper. If they didn't hit it, they would be sent back out into space, endlessly drifting farther away from Earth. Needless to say, the movie dramatized this part of the story with lots of intense music and build up, with viewers breathing a sigh of relief after the navigator hits the mark.

I believe many of us think walking in God's will is like hitting the mark the astronauts had to hit in their reentry. In our mind, it is as thin as a piece of paper, and we live in constant fear of missing it. But friends, if this were true, none of us would be able to enter the kingdom of God. We would be like the Israelites in Numbers, roaming the wilderness because of our stubbornness and doubt.

God wants us to come off the mountain of doubt and take the land. He promises to guide us beside the still waters, in green pastures filled with his peace. Let's put aside our limiting mentalities about who he is and walk in the abundance he provides.

DISCUSSION QUESTIONS

1. Do you ever think of God's will as a multiple-choice test? If so, how do you think this view affects your faith and decision-making?

2. In this chapter, we talked about how sheep are not stationary animals and must move to enjoy the abundant pasture Jesus refers to in John 10. What is one decision you've been putting off? If possible, set a date for when you will make this decision, and then ask God to open your eyes to ways he guides you after you take the first step.

3. As we make decisions, God grows our faith and ability to discern his voice in our lives. How have you seen this truth in your own life? Was there a specific decision you had to make where God deepened your understanding of his voice and his leading?

6

what to do when the instructions aren't clear

All arrows pointed to one simple fact: We needed to leave South Carolina. But I didn't want to admit it. This place had been my home for as long as I'd been breathing, and I didn't know anything different.

Aside from my family living less than five minutes from our house, I knew all the best places to eat. If you wanted wings, you went to D's. If you wanted Sunday brunch after church and some upscale Southern cooking, you went downtown to Motor Supply. Would the place we moved to even have Southern food? My guess was no; and if they did, it wouldn't be good.

Persistent questions consumed my mind, and I didn't have answers to any of them. Where would we go? How would I survive without my family?

My husband and I had been married for five months, and for most of that time, he'd commuted over four hours each day to get to and from work. Due to the relocation of production at the company where he worked, work travel became a daily necessity. And for various reasons, moving to the town where his company had relocated was not an option. So, the job hunt began. For months, he looked for work within our state. Then, the tristate area. After nine months of searching produced nothing, he told me, "I need to widen my search." I knew he was right, but my heart sank.

This was 2007, and neither of us had LinkedIn or Facebook. After our conversation, my husband updated his resume on a job site called Monster and made it searchable nationwide. I expected to wait weeks to months before hearing anything, but within twenty-four hours, he received a phone call. According to the manager on the other end of the phone, he was the perfect fit for a job they needed to fill as soon as possible. He wanted him to fly out for an interview the following week. As my husband relayed the news, everything sounded promising, as though our prayers were being answered. There was only one caveat. The job was located over 2,200 miles away, in northern Utah.

Sometimes God asks us to take a step into the unknown, but the only clear direction he gives us is "Go." He doesn't tell us what the next step is. He doesn't tell us where we'll end up or what we'll need to take with us along the way. But one instruction is clear: He doesn't want us to stay where we are.

Sometimes God asks us to take a step into the unknown, but the only clear direction he gives us is "Go."

This is the place of faith where my husband and I lived for several weeks as he flew west, went through an intense interview process, and talked to his anxious wife on the phone. But here's the thing: I don't like ambiguity. I'm sure you don't either. If I'm going to take a step into something unfamiliar, I want clear instructions telling me where to stay, what to take with me, and what to look out for. I want to know all the details and contingencies so I can create a backup plan. These clear instructions make me feel safe and like, somehow, these plans are going to foolproof my progress. Utah was about as unfamiliar to me as it got. But instead of giving me those foolproof instructions I asked for, God asked me to trust him.

Over the course of the next few weeks, God's guidance was obvious. He wanted us to move west. But we didn't know much more than that. I kept coming to him, wanting him to give me more information; but instead, he revealed one step. And then another. Each one was unveiled in his timing, but not before we needed to take it.

When I think of men and women God asked to step into the unknown, none are more prominent than Abram, who later became Abraham.

> *The* LORD *had said to Abram, "Go from your country, your people and your father's household to the land I will show you.*
>
> *"I will make you into a great nation,*
> *and I will bless you;*
> *I will make your name great,*
> *and you will be a blessing.*
> *I will bless those who bless you,*
> *and whoever curses you I will curse;*
> *and all peoples on earth*
> *will be blessed through you."* (Gen. 12:1–3)

Wait a minute, what? If I were Abraham, my mind would be reeling with questions, like "How will I know when I get there? What will the family I'm leaving behind do without me? What does this land look like?" Abraham had a clear command from God and the promise of a future inheritance, but he didn't have step-by-step instructions before leaving the land of Ur. His faith in the One who saw the path ahead of him had to guide him instead of a need for answers.

Even though Abraham didn't carry out his assignment perfectly, he did what God told him to do. If he had questions, we don't see them here. He chose to focus on God's Word more than any uncertainty or apprehension he felt. We see this response from Abraham in the next verse. He didn't ask for more information. Instead, he obeyed.

> *So Abram went, as the Lord had told him; and Lot went with him. Abram was seventy-five years old when he set out from Harran.* (Gen. 12:4)

Limited Information Can Protect Us

As I look back on the season of life when I left my hometown, I see God's mercy. Even though I didn't realize it at the time, the limited information we had was a form of protection. I didn't see the future trials and hardships we would walk through together. I didn't realize we would have to vacate the temporary housing Chris's employer provided in only a few days, due to a misunderstanding. And by not knowing these things, I felt a peace I wouldn't have felt otherwise.

If Chris and I had known our house in South Carolina would sit on the market for months without a buyer, we might have second-guessed our decision. If we had known we would be sleeping on an air mattress in a run-down rental with no other furniture, we would've questioned whether we'd been mistaken about God's guidance. As each new development unfolded, God guided us and provided for our needs, but he didn't give us insights into the future.

In Chapter One, we talked about the distorted perception of knowledge we take, and how we think more information will give us more freedom. But often, this is not the case. On the contrary, it frequently leads to inertia and decision fatigue. The more knowledge we obtain, the more we question what we already know. But there's another misconception we have in our endless quest for information and detailed instructions from God. We think it will give us peace. However, this perception of knowledge is often untrue, especially when it means knowledge of the future. Because when we obtain information before we're ready to receive it, it leads not to peace but to anxiety.

I look at God's call to Abraham and think about all the ways history unfolded over the next books of the Bible. Four books of the Bible are written between when God calls Abraham and when Joshua leads the Israelites into the promised land. The bulk of these books is filled with two things: wandering in the wilderness and the delivery of God's law, orchestrated through Moses. Moses puts up quite an argument when God first calls him to lead the Israelites out of Egypt, but I wonder how much longer his argument would've extended if he'd seen the future. If he'd known he would spend the next forty years in the wilderness, would he have questioned God more? Would he have been obedient? Moses is described as the humblest man on the face of the earth, but he had his limitations.

Over 1,500 years after the call of Moses, Jesus is in the land God promised. He is in the midst of his earthly ministry, performing miracles and teaching everyone who will listen. Even those who listen only with their ears and not their hearts follow him around, and he tells them the truth he came to deliver, straight from the Father. In the passage we've been exploring together, John 10, he makes another bold statement. Jews surround him at the Festival of Dedication and push him to declare he is the Messiah. Jesus's response is one he makes repeatedly throughout the book of John. "The works I do in my Father's name testify about me." But then he goes a step further and adds, "But you do not believe because you are not my sheep" (John 10:25–26).

There's a lot here, so let's take some time to unpack these words. The more we understand what Jesus is telling the Pharisees, the more we will be able to see how these same principles apply to us today in our search for guidance and truth. First, Jesus tells the Jews his works testify to who he is. Throughout the book of John, Jesus has performed countless miracles and has done everything his Father asked him to do. His works identify him as the Messiah, the promised one they've been waiting for, but the Pharisees don't see this. They want more. They want him to "tell them plainly" as they say numerous times, even though he's already told them and they don't believe. Do you see a correlation here?

As much as I dislike admitting it, I am sometimes like these Pharisees. In my need for security, I ask him to give me more. More guidance and instruction. More clarity. I reason that by doing this, I will ensure my ability to follow God's will. But if I dig deeper and ask myself some hard questions, my underlying motivation is a lack of trust. Like the Pharisees, I'm asking him to prove who he is, to tell me plainly, even though he's already shown me who he is numerous times.

If I look back at the work of Jesus in my life, his identity is clear. His faithfulness is evident. Much of the time when I'm hesitant to go in a direction he's provided, I don't need more validation of his leading; I simply need to pay attention to what he's already done. This is what will keep me moving forward in the safe pasture he provides for his sheep. My faith in his character will keep me from falling for the lies of the Enemy, who comes to kill, steal, and destroy.

In the second half of this verse, Jesus makes another distinction. He says the reason the Pharisees don't believe is because they aren't his sheep. This is a tough statement to read, but it is also where the correlation between us, dear readers, and the Pharisees ends. Because if we've declared him as Lord of our lives, we *are* his sheep. We belong to him. To experience the gifts of the pasture he leads us into and live life to the full, we need to remember who our Shepherd is. He is not a Shepherd who leads us into the pasture and then abandons us to the wolves. He is not a Shepherd who leaves the pasture and expects us to have all the answers. He is the Shepherd who stays, who guides us and intercedes for us. He never stops.

> He is not a Shepherd who leaves the pasture and expects us to have all the answers. He is the Shepherd who stays, who guides us and intercedes for us. He never stops.

Is Trust Our Motivation, or Is It Control?

I need more instruction because I want to carry out God's will correctly. I need more guidance because I want to make sure I'm on the right track. Have you ever told yourself these things? I know I have. And because we serve a gracious, merciful God, he often gives what we ask for. He sends a friend to tell us what we need to hear at the exact right moment. Or he uses a book we're reading to confirm what he told us and give us confidence in our path.

But other times, he waits. He holds back on the repeated signs and confirmations. Not because he's angry or distant, but because he wants to see how we'll respond. Will we trust him to provide for us, even when we're still uncertain about what he's asked us to do? Will our faith in who he is go beyond what he does for us?

The truth is, when we have detailed, step-by-step guidelines laid out before us along with Siri telling us when to stop, go, and detour, we rely on God less and less. Self-sufficiency becomes our companion instead of our Father, and we think to ourselves, "I've got this." On the other hand, when we have limited information, it can lead to either anxiety or humility.

Do you remember the missionary couple to East Africa we talked about in the previous chapter? During their conversation, Randy talked about how Christianity was on the rise in Africa. So much so that there was an urgent need for pastors. One of Randy's key roles in his work was training pastors and providing them with resources to help them lead new churches. As he talked about the different challenges they faced, he emphasized how this work was a gift, and he felt privileged to be able to do it. Then he said another thing that stayed with me. He said these pastors said yes to the call to enter ministry with no training, no previous experience, and no knowledge of how they were going to carry out what was required. Some of them lived several bus rides from any type of facility where they could receive training, but they were willing to do whatever it took to spread the gospel message.

After hearing this, Pastor Tim asked whether it was a sense of obligation that motivated these new pastors or a true desire to be there. "To be honest, it's a little bit of both," Randy said. "But all of them want to be there. There's no one telling them they need to do this."

As I think back on this story, one singular thought overwhelms me. *This is the type of person I want to be.* I want to be the one who says yes out of a love for God and an urgency to spread his love to others he places in my path. I want my desire to be his messenger to be stronger than my need for more information, clarity, and answers. When he tells me to "go," I want my trust in him to lead me instead of being led by my doubts and fears.

How about you, friend? Is there an area of your life where you sense God saying "Go," but you're waiting for further instruction? Has your need for clarity kept you in a holding pattern, afraid to take a step forward? I get it. I know what it's like to spend months questioning God, only to realize he was waiting for me to follow Abraham's example and believe him. Here are three key questions to ask ourselves when God nudges us to move but we're uncertain of any direction beyond that.

What is the benefit of staying where I am? This is a question I ask coaching clients often. The reason why this question is effective is because it forces us to evaluate our motivation and inner thought life. Sometimes, what motivates us to stay where we are is comfort and familiarity. It is the security of knowing that if we keep the status quo, we maintain a sense of control. Or at least we think we do. Other times, it's the belief that our progress has to be perfect. But friend, as we've explored before, there is no such thing as perfect progress. There is progress *with* the One who is perfect, and there is staying where we are.

Sometimes staying where we are is the best option for our current season. There have been times when Chris and I wanted to move, but when we sought God's guidance, all arrows told us to remain put. The benefit of staying where we were was peace and obedience; but we had to be still, shut out the noise, and seek God to arrive at this conclusion.

Am I motivated by my desire for God or my desire for control? I realize this is a pointed question. To be honest, it makes me uncomfortable. But it's a question we need to ask ourselves because our motivation is the key to everything.

Many times, when I've asked myself this question, the answer was control. Once I realized this truth, I dug a bit deeper and asked myself, "Do answers and instructions really give me control?" The answer was no. Instructions may give me the illusion of control and sometimes give me a sense of confidence, but most of the time the outcome is out of my hands. I can still mess things up, even with the most explicit steps a, b, and c. Something I don't foresee could happen, and I would be unprepared for how to handle the situation or how to respond. When there are other people involved, any sense of control becomes even more of an illusion because I'm not dealing with robots, and I'm sure you aren't either.

On the other hand, when my desire is for more of God, he always delivers. He may show up in a way I don't expect or in a different way than I ask for, but he always shows up. He doesn't turn away when we seek him with a heart longing for more of his grace, truth, and wisdom. So one desire leads me to an illusion of control and never delivers, and the other one always delivers exactly what I need.

How has God prepared me to make this decision? When we're focused on the future, we often forget to look back on how God has led us to this point. But when we look back, we see all the ways God has directed us and prepared us to make the decision we now face. We may see the ways he equipped us to say yes and handle whatever our yes entails.

In the months leading up to our move to Utah, I looked back on the past year of our marriage. I remembered Chris telling me his work would probably require us to move at some point and discussing what this transition might look like. At the time, I put the conversation at the back of my mind and tried to ignore the possibility of uprooting our lives. But when I looked back, I realized God was preparing me in that moment. He was giving me an arrow, a sign of all the ways he would lead us before I even realized it.

When I shifted my perspective and saw God's hand in the details of our lives, I felt peace. And this peace kept me from obsessing about the future and all the unknowns. It kept me centered when questions about the details bombarded my mind.

Several weeks ago, a friend shared a quote from Oswald Chambers with me. In his beautiful, succinct prose, Chambers describes the tension between certainty and uncertainty.

> *Certainty is the mark of the commonsense life: gracious uncertainty is the mark of the spiritual life. To be certain of God means that we are uncertain in all our ways, we do not know what the day may bring forth. This is generally said with a sigh of sadness, it should be rather an expression of breathless expectation. We are uncertain of the next step, but we are certain of God.*[1]

Friend, this is a lifelong process, and one we will never master in this lifetime. But the effort is worth it. The tension we feel between grasping this life and releasing our grip is worth it. And in the moments when we do realize the gift of letting God be God, we see his ways are better than ours. I can think of no better example of this way of living than Paul, who in his letter to the Philippians said, "Not that I have already obtained all this, or have already arrived at my goal, but I press on to take hold of that for which Christ Jesus took hold of me" (Phil. 3:12).

Before Jesus met Paul on the road to Damascus, Paul followed guidelines better than anyone. Like many of us, they were his source of assurance and surety. If there was a rulebook to follow, he checked off every item on it. But after his conversion, he considered all of that rubbish (Phil. 3:8). He traded his security in the law for a security that can only be found in knowing Christ. Knowing him became his ultimate goal and his only hope.

The more I journey through this life, the more I realize Paul had a deep level of spiritual understanding that most of us only dream about. But at the same time, I want to strive toward this life he displayed, completely undone by my love and dedication to my Savior. Perhaps you do too?

As we face decisions and unknowns today and in the days ahead, let's remember Paul's example. When we're tempted to place our security in instructions and answers, let's recall his words. Christ "took hold" of us for the joy set before him: a forever union with you and me. And even in our questions, he continues to take hold of us now.

DISCUSSION QUESTIONS

1. Have you ever received guidance from God that didn't seem to make sense? How did you respond? What did the experience teach you about God's voice?

2. In this chapter, we talked about three questions we can ask ourselves when God asks us to "go" but we're unsure of any direction beyond that. One of the questions was "What is the benefit of staying where you are?" How would you answer this question?

3. Throughout the book of John, Jesus tells the Jews that his works testify about who he is. This is a good reminder for us all when we ask God to give us another sign. Instead, we can look back and see what he's done. How have his works testified to who he is in your life?

7

when fear masks itself as discernment

When I reached the front of the sanctuary, a wall of people blocked my view. I couldn't see the woman who called out to the congregation offering prayer. To be honest, I felt silly standing there, not having anyone to pray with. I almost turned around and walked back to my seat.

It's what she had said moments before that kept me there. She'd named my exact need during this difficult season.

I lingered for what felt like an eternity with my eyes closed but a mind too busy to pray. Then I opened my eyes just enough to see if the wall of people was still there. It was. I was about to turn around and go back to my seat, but I felt a hand grasp my arm. Without seeing her, I knew it was Kim, the woman who offered prayer. She pulled me through the crowd of others surrounding me.

As I shared my burden and need with this person I barely knew, I sensed her compassion. She prayed over me and named weights I didn't even know I was carrying. I felt seen. Relief that only comes from the release of an invisible burden filled me.

But seconds before this intimate time with God, I'd been ready to run. I'd wanted to make a beeline back to my seat under the shadow of others standing there and the covering of dim lights. What I couldn't see almost kept me from standing at the altar with a belief that God had a reason for me to be there. To receive the gift, my faith in the middle of the unknown had to outweigh my fear of uncertainty. Even if just for a moment.

Until this point in my life, I was usually the watcher during these altar call moments. I stood back, sang worship songs, and observed. Sometimes I closed my eyes and prayed. But to walk up front felt too risky. Even if I felt the Spirit nudge me forward, I questioned. God has coaxed me past many of my fears in this area, but sometimes I still hesitate. *Other people up there need prayer more than I do*, I'd think. Or, *What will people think? Will my teenage son be worried, thinking his mom is on the brink of a mental breakdown?*

For decades of my life, these fears often masked themselves as something else—discernment. If I didn't understand a spiritual experience or it made me uncomfortable, I convinced myself it wasn't needed or real. To be honest, my perspective was jaded by church hurt and abusive leadership, and I thought the prophesying, laying on of hands, and speaking in tongues seemed like a lot of theatrics. If it was real, it was in a dimension I didn't understand.

With time and much prayer seeking God's wisdom, I realized I would never fully understand God or what is taking place in the unseen realm. And that is okay. Because the point where I think I can understand all of God's ways is the end of humility. Humility is the vessel he uses to deliver understanding, not pride. So instead of letting fear and arrogance be my guide, I ask him to open my eyes. I ask for his help to put aside my jaded thinking and be open to receive whatever his Spirit wants to speak to me.

Sometimes, I still mess it up. I think I'm exercising discernment and wisdom when I'm being led by fear. But the more I seek God in this area, the more he shows me the difference between these two motivations. So how do we know? What does true discernment look like, and how do we know when we're being led by its adversary, fear? Over the years, I've learned a few key ways to tell the difference.

Discernment versus Fear: How to Know the Difference

In the Bible, Paul tells us discernment is a spiritual gift and it is valuable to those who exercise it. It keeps the church from falling prey to false doctrine or false prophets and alerts us when God's Word is being taken out of context. Then, in 1 Corinthians, Paul states another key truth about discernment.

> *The person without the Spirit does not accept the things that come from the Spirit of God but considers them foolishness, and cannot understand them because they are discerned only through the Spirit. The person with the Spirit makes judgments about all things, but such a person is not subject to merely human judgments, for,*
>
> *"Who has known the mind of the Lord*
> *so as to instruct him?"*
>
> *But we have the mind of Christ.* (1 Cor. 2:14–16)

This verse leads us to our first way of knowing whether we're led by fear or discernment.

Fear is often propelled by a lack of understanding, but discernment is an understanding that comes from the Spirit.

When we don't understand something, one of our natural reactions is to flee. We gravitate toward things that make us feel safe and comfortable. But friends, the Holy Spirit cannot be confined by our comfort zone. We can't expect to understand what God is doing in people's hearts and lives with our finite human brains. It is only through the Holy Spirit revealing his heart to us and opening our eyes that we will grasp, even on a tiny level, his work and his ways. But often, our temptation is to focus on the seen and the temporary. We focus on what we know.

We see examples of this mindset when Paul travels to Athens to preach the gospel and is dismayed to see many of the inhabitants worshiping false gods and falling prey to a religion of superstition. Instead of following the one true God, who did not need a created vessel to be close to his people, they followed religions filled with meaningless rituals meant to enslave people.

When they hear Paul's teaching, they question him, saying, "May we learn about this new teaching you are presenting? Because what you say sounds strange to us, and we want to know what these things mean." While this request seems promising, the text goes on to say, "Now all the Athenians and the foreigners residing there spent their time on nothing else but telling or hearing something new" (Acts 17:19–21 CSB).

The Athenians were not led by a desire for truth but a desire for knowledge. And as we've stated throughout this book, knowledge alone will never lead to the freedom God desires for us. They were led by a desire for new ideas to debate and discuss with each other. Unfortunately, this lack of understanding kept many of them from receiving the truth Paul preached in Athens. Like so many of us do when we see or hear something that makes us uncomfortable, they fled. But because of God's grace and a discernment that only comes from his Spirit, some of them joined Paul and believed (Acts 17:34).

These Athenians who joined Paul and exercised faith realized an amazing truth about the works of God: The fact that something makes us uncomfortable doesn't make it untrue. In fact, the Holy Spirit does some of his best work when we're stretched beyond what we know. When we leave behind what's familiar and walk with him into the unknown. This is what faith is.

> The fact that something makes us uncomfortable doesn't make it untrue.

Fear comes from a reliance on self, but discernment comes from reliance on God. When I focus on myself and my own prejudices, experience, and pride, fear will lead. And friends, just to clarify, I'm not talking about a healthy fear that keeps us from making rash decisions or from climbing into the car with a stalker. I'm talking about faith-squelching fear. This type of fear keeps us stuck in our strongholds and prevents us from believing God has anything better for us. It keeps the church from being the "city on a hill" Matthew described in his Gospel (Matt. 5:14).

Throughout our key passage in John 10, Jesus equates his followers with sheep, which are notoriously unintelligent animals. Their natural inclination is to follow a leader, and they will do so even if it leads to their harm or death. As I researched these characteristics, I came across a BBC article showing the extent of the sheep's dedication to following someone or something. In Turkey, more than 1,500 sheep fell off a forty-nine-foot-high cliff. This accident resulted in the death of four hundred, who cushioned the fall of the others who survived. Why did this happen? Because one sheep walked off the cliff, and the others followed.[1]

While sheep falling off cliffs is an extreme example, it illustrates a key truth Jesus emphasizes in this passage: When we follow someone or something other than our true leader, death will follow. Of course, most of the time, the death we experience will not be physical. It will be a spiritual death, a slow loss of our purpose and fullness of life. And following another leader includes following our fear. Discernment, on the other hand, can only come from complete and utter reliance on God.

If we look at references to discernment in Scripture, we see that it comes from God alone. No amount of speculation or reliance on ourselves will produce spiritual discernment. In Psalm 119, we see the writer precede his request for discernment with humility:

> *I am your servant; give me discernment*
> *that I may understand your statutes.* (Ps. 119:125)

The writer recognizes that a humble attitude and posture before the Lord is needed. Fear, on the other hand, is often the result of us trying to produce righteousness from our own works, which will get us nowhere. It is the product of comparing our spiritual life to someone else's and trying to elevate ourselves above them. But wisdom that comes from God teaches us we are all sinners in need of grace, and God gives it freely to those who confess their need for it.

Fear focuses on outward appearances, but discernment is propelled by a love for God and others. I can't tell you the number of times I've felt God nudge me to take action, but I've thought, *What will people think?* It's embarrassing to admit, but it's the honest truth. When we focus on our appearance and others' opinions, fear will lead us. It will whisper lies, telling us it's better to remain in our seats and not be the subject of raised eyebrows. But friends, the blessing is worth it. The gift is worth it. A few months ago, a friend shared a testimony with me at our women's Bible study and showed me how much we risk when we choose not to do what God is prompting us to do.

One of our church attendees, Adaia, is a local artist who occasionally paints during worship and the message. Her paintings depict what God is speaking to her heart during service, and she often shares the meaning of these paintings with us on social media during the following weeks. During one church service a couple of years ago, she began a picture of a rosebud, almost ready to blossom, in full color. But for a reason she couldn't pinpoint, she felt prompted to sit down before the end of the sermon instead of finishing the painting. She wasn't sure why, but after seeking the Lord in prayer, she realized he wanted her to give the painting away to someone in the congregation.

As she prayed and watched attendees come to the altar, one person caught her attention. Katie stood at the front, helping another woman in our church family with her children. Katie and her husband had been trying to start a family for years, but so far, they hadn't been able to conceive. Adaia knew at that moment that Katie was the person God wanted her to give the painting to, but she didn't know when or how.

After much prayer, Adaia reached out to Katie on Facebook and asked if she'd like to have coffee. Even though Katie barely knew Adaia, she agreed. They met during the week, and Adaia brought the painting with her. Without knowing all the details of Katie's story, she sat across the table and spoke the words the Lord had given her, "Your wait is over." Needless to say, Katie wept.

The following month, Katie and her husband discovered their wait was indeed over. Katie was pregnant, and nine months later she gave birth to a healthy baby girl.

As I listened to Katie tell this amazing story, here's what I kept thinking: Adaia could've easily let fear lead her. She could've worried about how she would look to this person she barely knew and ignored the nudge from God. After all, can you imagine if she had prophesied this to Katie and it hadn't come true? That was the last thing she wanted, and it could've made her appear foolish or uncaring. But instead, she let her love for God and for the church body lead her. Because of this love, both women have beautiful testimonies to share with others.

> The Spirit of God will never tell us to be self-serving and self-focused.

If we focus on ourselves and our appearance, we don't have to ask ourselves whether discernment is leading us. It isn't. The Spirit of God will never tell us to be self-serving and self-focused. He prompts us to be brave, to be bold, and to go places we may have never planned for ourselves. And when we do, we will witness miracles and encounters we never knew to hope for. We will see that the God we serve is truly the God of the impossible, and we get to be part of it. If we'll only listen and move with him.

True Discernment Comes from Death to Self

Even though Jesus's words in John 10 apply to us as his followers, it's also important to remember his audience. As we discussed in earlier chapters, he was speaking to the Pharisees. So why is it important for him to tell the Pharisees his followers will come, go, and find pasture? While there are many different reasons Jesus could have made this distinction, one stands out. The Pharisees lived bound by a set of man-made rules and focused on outward appearances, but they did not know true freedom. Instead, they were bound by their suspicions. If you look at the history of Israel, you can see why.

The Pharisees often get a bad rap, and with good reason. They are the only group of people in the Gospels that Jesus refers to as "sons of hell" (Matt. 23:15 NASB). But if we look at the history of these spiritual leaders, we see a past filled with trauma. Their nation, Israel, had strayed away from God and, due to their sin, had been taken into captivity. There was a strong influence from Greek culture, and many Jews abandoned their beliefs to adopt pagan rituals. The Pharisees' goal was to stand against this influence from culture and preserve Mosaic law. In fact, they are likely the reason why the Torah was not destroyed.

Although their original intentions were good, the Pharisees lost sight of what mattered. They turned from preserving Mosaic law and began adding to it. They were led by a sense of nationalism and loyalty to their culture rather than being led by the Spirit of God. And despite their fortitude in preserving the law, they failed to see when the fulfillment of it stood right in front of them. They were led not by true discernment that comes from God but by fear. Fear of what they didn't understand. Fear of being exposed. After seeing Jesus's abilities and hearing his teachings, they knew he could take power away from them and bring the hollow doctrine they preached to light. Once they realized this, nearly every interaction they had with Jesus was to manipulate him or trick him into doing something that contradicted Scripture.

Contrary to the doctrine the Pharisees preached, Jesus taught a gospel that broke the chains of religion and empty rituals. When Jesus described his sheep, he illustrated a freedom that can only come from him. But the Pharisees were unable to understand this because they were not led by the Spirit of God. While they may have thought they were practicing discernment and being wise, they were doing the exact opposite.

Scripture shows this type of interaction with the Pharisees was an ongoing theme throughout not only this Gospel but others as well. As I studied many of these conversations, one instance struck me. Why? Because Jesus defines what discernment is. This defining moment takes place in John 7, where the Pharisees are once again trying to entrap Jesus, who has just healed a blind man on the Sabbath. Jesus points out their double standard, saying that they circumcise on the Sabbath.

Then Jesus defines what discernment truly is: "Do not judge by appearances, but judge with right judgment" (John 7:24 ESV). If there was ever a definition of what we're seeking in this chapter, this is it. But what is right judgment? Clearly, it is the exact opposite of the judgment the Pharisees were practicing.

Craig S. Keener explains this concept further in his New Testament commentary on John:

> *They are observing the letter of the law, but do not understand what the law is really about, neither in its witness to Jesus nor in its goal of expressing God's own love and mercy in the life of God's people. Making a right judgment (he dikaia krisis) is dependent on seeking God's will and not one's own (5:30). They lack this disposition; they are too shallow. They have no depth in themselves and thus cannot recognize God at work among them. God himself is the one who is dikaios ("right," "righteous"; cf. Jn 17:25; 1 Jn 2:29; 3:7; Rev 16:5), so their lack of right judgment is yet another indication not only of their law breaking but of their alienation from God.*
>
> *This call to right judgment is a challenge to each of us, for we are all guilty at times of judging by appearances. The only way to avoid such shallowness is to be united with God and to share in his truth about Jesus and about our own lives. This requires that we will God's will (7:17), which means God's will as God knows*

> *it, not as our prejudices and sins tailor it. To will God's will is to have a purity of heart and a clarity of vision that come through death to self. Until we have found our own heart (which lies deeper than our emotions and imagination) and made contact with God there, we will be in danger of judging by appearances instead of with right judgment.*[2]

True discernment comes from a desire to know, love, and obey God. It leads us when this desire exceeds our desire for comfort and stagnant living. It means putting aside what the world has taught us to value and seeking what God values. And friends, what God values most is people. He values relationships and wants to see others know and love him too.

We can never know if we are being led by true discernment without examining our hearts. Asking ourselves some honest questions is a good place to start.

1. What is my motivation?
2. What am I afraid of?
3. Am I being led by my love for God and others or by a focus on myself?

But asking these questions is only the beginning. We must let God into those places in our hearts where we've held on to fear, past hurt, and a jaded view of his bride, the church. Only he can transform us, and this transformation starts with an invitation. If you're unsure what to pray, these words from David are a simple, beautiful appeal to the God who hears us:

> *Search me, God, and know my heart;*
> *test me and know my anxious thoughts.*
> *See if there is any offensive way in me,*
> *and lead me in the way everlasting.* (Ps. 139:23–24)

If we pray this prayer with a heart open to receive whatever God has for us, amazing things happen.

Where True Discernment Leads Us

When I walked to the front of that sanctuary to receive prayer several years ago, I was grappling with another long season of postpartum depression. This sister in Christ said God was reaching out his hand toward me and all I had to do was take hold. Much like the invitation to climb on my husband's motorcycle many years ago, all he wanted was my yes. In other seasons of life, my mind would've responded with something sarcastic like, "Yeah, but is he really? Because it sure doesn't feel like it." But in that moment, I knew God was speaking to me through this woman. His love was as tangible as the tears falling down my face. He knew my need, but he also knew I was terrified.

I'm so glad I didn't let fear keep me in my seat. Instead, I said yes to the uncertainty. I said yes to standing there at the altar and feeling foolish. And it was the best decision I made the year after my daughter was born.

Why? Because when I walked out of the sanctuary, I was changed. My countenance was lighter. I could breathe again. And the reason was as simple as it was profound: I shared my burden with someone else. Instead of trying to carry it on my own or acting as though it didn't exist, I said it out loud. My friend read between the words and knew that my unspoken question was "This is me, baggage and all. Will you love me despite the fact that I don't have it all together?" And the answer was "Yes."

Discernment that comes from the Spirit will always lead us straight to the heart of the Father. It reveals his heart to us in our weariness, our questions, and even our doubt. And his heart for us is perfect, untainted love.

DISCUSSION QUESTIONS

1. In this chapter, we unpacked some key differences between fear and discernment. What are some other differences you would add? How do you think discernment that comes from the Holy Spirit is different from fear?

2. One of the reasons we are often led by fear is because of a lack of understanding. Has there ever been a time when a misunderstanding caused you or someone close to you to react in fear? If you encountered a similar situation now, would you react differently? How so?

3. David's words in Psalm 139:23–24 are a beautiful prayer we can adapt for ourselves to invite the transformation of the Holy Spirit. Read this prayer out loud. What stands out to you the most?

8

is it a closed door or a distraction?

When my daughter was two, she developed a fear of all animals. Not just large or vicious ones, but all animals. Our family was considering adopting a puppy, but this change in our daughter gave us pause. It had been a couple of years since our other dog passed, and we were ready to bring another one into the home. But we wondered if Elise would be okay. Was this decision a mistake? In the end, we decided we didn't want to feed this newfound anxiety. So when we found a lab mix at a local humane society and the rest of our family fell in love with him, we moved forward.

For several weeks, our home was filled with loud screaming. My blood pressure was at an all-time high, and I wondered if we'd made a mistake. On more than one occasion, I considered returning the dog to his foster home. And before you're tempted to judge me, let me tell you something about my daughter. She has a scream with decibels that have been known to shatter glass.

But whenever I thought about putting the dog in the back of our SUV, I remembered what the humane society had told us: Our home was his fourth. After spending a few weeks or months at several other homes before ours, he was returned to the foster parents with comments saying he was "too rambunctious" or "too high energy." This poor pup had never known stability or a forever home, and I was determined to give him both.

Around the fourth week, our daughter made a turn. My husband let her give Baxter treats and would hold her while she rubbed his back. The next week, she let him lick her face. Each day, she grew more comfortable with this dog who was bigger than she was, and within two months, she was bossing him around like the alpha I knew she was.

As I look at our big black lab mix today and think of all the joy he's brought to our family, I can't imagine life without him. He greets my firstborn every day when he returns home from school. He joins us on family hikes and swims in the river when the weather turns warm. But during those first few weeks with him, I questioned our decision. It was a choice we had prayed over and entered with much thought and insight, but I second-guessed it nonetheless.

When we make decisions and encounter difficulties, how do we know the difference between a closed door and a distraction? We want to honor God and make choices that will help us and our families thrive. We know we aren't guaranteed a trouble-free life, and growth often happens after encountering tough circumstances. But how do we know when God is signaling us to walk away? Is there a way to discern whether something is worth pursuing, despite the obstacles and struggles? I believe there is, but it requires the renewal of our minds. We have to look beyond the troubles we face at the moment and ask ourselves, "Where do I want to go?" We'll talk more about this later.

Sometimes we hit a roadblock or detour after following what we believed to be God's leading. Then we ask, "Was that really God?" We think the struggle is a signal to retreat, but what if it's a sign to keep going? What if it's a sign that our enemy doesn't want us to experience whatever it is God has for us and that he and his armies are trying to distract us by using whatever means possible?

You may be facing far more dire circumstances than a screaming toddler who is afraid of your new dog. I get that. I don't want to make light of any hardship you may be facing or imply there's anything easy about it.

Perhaps you're facing an unwanted diagnosis. You thought God was opening the door for treatment with the promise to heal, but a second opinion is making you second-guess your options. Or maybe a job opportunity opened up after months of searching. You were ready to accept the offer, but then you found out the work requires more hours and demands on your time than you expected.

As we discussed in previous chapters, Jesus said his sheep would come, go, and find pasture. Using a shepherding analogy his listeners would understand, Jesus speaks to the abundant nature of his guidance. He does not withhold his goodness from us when we seek his guidance. If an obstacle is in our path, we do not need to assume it is from God.

> What if distractions can be holy moments? What if instead of obstructions to our path, we viewed them as invitations to transform and renew our minds?

Rather than retreat or go in the opposite direction when we encounter these unexpected obstructions, we have a Guide. Jesus described him as our Advocate and our Counselor. But I think that often, we act as though he isn't there. We have a preconceived notion in our minds of how things will play out, and if our situation veers from this set path, we walk away. Sometimes, we don't even consult God to determine if this disturbance to our plans is from him. We assume it isn't, and we call it quits. What if distractions can be holy moments? What if instead of obstructions to our path, we viewed them as invitations to transform and renew our minds?

The Test and Approve Method

In Romans 12:2, Paul tells us this world has a pattern. He exhorts us not to conform to it, but heeding this instruction requires a transformation on our part. Here's the thing about patterns. As humans, we're prone to habits, which are a form of a pattern. A basic one might include waking up at the sound of your alarm, sliding your feet into your slippers, and brushing your teeth. We form habits, or patterns, to deal with the problems and complexities of life, and we can follow one without even realizing it.

In my prayer life, my pattern sometimes looks like this:

1. Make plans and develop habits for the future I desire.
2. Consult God about the plans where I need his help.
3. Praise God when I see a visible answer to my prayer, and if I don't, do things to change the situation myself.

Now, here's the problem. While there's nothing inherently wrong with any of these steps, they're shortsighted. If I'm only focusing on what I can see right now in the physical world, I often miss what God is trying to teach me or reveal to my spirit. My character will remain shallow and results-driven instead of becoming steadfast and faithful despite my momentary struggle. If these steps become the pattern I follow in my prayer life every time a situation gets difficult, I will miss the beautiful transformation God wants to enact in me.

When Paul writes his letter to the early Christians in Rome, he points out the intentionality each of us must practice in our daily lives with God.

> *Do not conform to the pattern of this world, but be transformed by the renewing of your mind. Then you will be able to test and approve what God's will is—his good, pleasing and perfect will.* (Rom. 12:2)

Let's examine the latter part of this verse for a moment because it contains an assurance we often overlook. I know I did for many years, but this affirmation from Paul helps us think in a fresh, new way about God's will in our lives.

By renewing my mind rather than conforming to the pattern of this world, I am able to discern what many of us see as elusive or mysterious: God's will. Instead of staying stuck in a cycle of hesitation and wondering whether a word I received is from God, I can "test and approve it." I can move forward with confidence, even when there are distractions or disruptions to my plans.

So how do we achieve this transformation? How do we renew our minds in a world where we're bombarded with messages telling us we need to look out for ourselves? Patterns or habits are effective because once we adopt them, we follow them without even thinking about them. When you flip the light switch each morning, you're not thinking about why. The room is dark, and you know what will resolve this problem.

If we want to stop our conformity to the world's pattern, we must replace it with a new one. The pattern that feeds my flesh must be transformed into a pattern that renews my mind and my spirit. This starts with an honest assessment of our lives and the areas where we're prone to adopt a short-term view of our circumstances.

Let's use the disruption to our dreams or plans as an example. We pray to God about a specific situation, and he prompts us to act. Following his leading, we move forward. Then something unexpected happens. The clear path we envisioned turns out to be a mirage, and we encounter obstacles that can look a million different ways. Is it a closed door or a distraction? Following a new, Spirit-led pattern, we ask ourselves these questions:

Have I prayed to God and asked him to either remove the obstacle or give me strength to persist through it? What was the result? Even if God doesn't remove the obstacle, he often gives peace in the middle of it. He will also help us to see new ways he's working in our situation, ways we often don't expect or anticipate. Now, if we're experiencing constant anxiety or inner emotional turmoil and peace is nowhere to be found, this may be a sign that we need to draw a boundary or close a door. God does not want us to sacrifice our physical and emotional health on the altar of pride. But he does want to grow us up, and sometimes this means persisting through discomfort.

How might your resolve and persistence through this obstacle grow not only your faith but the faith of others who are watching? When Jesus talks about his sheep grazing in abundant pastures in John 10, he's not referring to a life where we'll stay in the same place forever and simply eat the grass of his field. "Life to the full" does not equal a stagnant life or a life where we'll never face obstacles. If we're never prompted to step outside our area of familiarity, we don't grow. What we view as a closed door is often God's way of refining us into followers who are relentless in our pursuit of his call on our lives. Although the troubles we face may seem detrimental to our progress, one day we will look back and see them as moments when God moved in ways only he could.

> What we view as a closed door is often God's way of refining us into followers who are relentless in our pursuit of his call on our lives.

Remember, the struggles we face aren't simply about us. Others are watching our journey too. When they see God move through a seemingly impossible situation, they're often prompted to take steps of faith they wouldn't have taken otherwise. Our faithfulness becomes an invitation for them to respond to God's call and step into the unknown.

To overcome this obstacle or struggle, does God have to intervene in a way only he can? Sometimes we encounter situations where unless God moves, the hurdles will be impossible to surmount. He places us in this position so that we will not only call on him but witness the miracle. Often, others will too. As we share our testimony and invite others to be part of what God is doing, revival can happen.

But if our faith relies solely on our skill sets and experiences, and we don't have to test the limits, we also won't have the opportunity to watch God move in miraculous ways. Our view of God will stay inside the box we've placed him in, and we won't see how vast and powerful he truly is.

* * *

While there are many other questions we could add to this list, these help us to think beyond the here and now. They cause us to consider how God is shaping not only today but the future we have in him because God isn't as concerned with our momentary comfort as he is with the person we're becoming. These circumstances we perceive as open or closed doors go far beyond what we see in the present. Author and speaker Lisa

Whittle explains this concept of spiritual doors in her book, *God Knows*, and illustrates how we can misconstrue God's intention.

> *Doors are deeply significant in Scripture. They are mentioned roughly four hundred times throughout the Old and New Testaments in both literal and figurative ways. But it's not just about doors as opportunities or non-opportunities—relegated to a mode of communication from God. The concept of the door was, in Scripture, those things as well. But it also represented much more—freedom, faith, and judgment, to name a few.*
>
> *Get ready, because here's where it gets good.*
>
> *In the most incredible mention of a door in Scripture, Christ calls Himself a door in John 10:9: "I am the door. If anyone enters by me, he will be saved and will go in and out and find pasture" (ESV).*[1]

Lisa goes on to say, "He *is* the door. He *is* the dream." I mean, can I get an amen? While we're perceiving open doors, closed doors, and everything in between, we forget that God himself is the fulfillment of our greatest needs and heart's desires. He doesn't want to be second to anything else. What we see as a closed door can be an invitation to a deeper understanding of who he is. It's also an opportunity to embrace the long-term work he's doing instead of obsessing over the obstacles we face right now.

Sometimes this long-term perspective requires a shift in where we're fixing our gaze. It requires us to move past the biggest distraction of all.

The Biggest Distraction of All

Last week I received an unexpected email. It was a follow-up to a job application I completed two months ago, and the hiring manager informed me that I'd made it to the second round in the process. I was elated but also confused. I had never expected the process to take so long and assumed they'd offered the position to someone else. After praying to God and asking him to open doors according to his will, I had concluded that this job must not be part of his plan for my future.

Now, this isn't just any job. It's the type of career I dreamed about in college when I completed my bachelor of arts degree. While I love writing books and articles, one of my greatest passions is editing. Helping other writers refine their work and release it out into the world brings me deep joy and satisfies a place in my soul that writing my own pieces doesn't. But when I approached my college adviser about pursuing editing jobs, he told me my grades weren't good enough. He said publishing companies wanted to see a 4.0 GPA, so for over twenty years, the girl who wanted to be an editor has been a distant memory. Until last week.

The end result of this application process is still unknown. I've made it to the next step, and I'm happy to know I'm still in the running. But weeks ago, I thought it was a done deal. I was already looking at other options for part-time remote work and picking Canva templates to update my resume.

Sometimes the biggest distraction to our persistence with God is waiting. Our culture doesn't like to wait, and each day we're given a reason not to. We can order our groceries online and skip the checkout line. When visiting Disney and other theme parks, there are lightning lanes and VIP upgrades to avoid long wait times.

None of us come to God with the desires of our hearts and say, "God, I really want this [insert desire], but if you want to make me wait a year or two, that's okay." And yet, over and over we see men and women of the Bible waiting for him to fulfill his promises. We see them persisting through years of silence, persecution, and trials before watching God intervene in ways only he could.

While there are several examples of barren women in Scripture who waited for God to answer their prayers for a child, Hannah's story is one of my favorites. Perhaps it's her humble spirit in the midst of mockery and rejection. And how many other mothers would give up their firstborn for the Lord's service after years of childlessness?

When we read the story of Hannah in Scripture, we're immediately told of the stigma that burdened her. She had no children. And as a Jewish woman living during the eleventh century BC, this was not a favorable situation. Not only was Hannah barren, but she was ridiculed by her husband's other wife, Peninnah. Year after year, Peninnah reminded Hannah of her affliction.

But Hannah did not become bitter or resentful toward God in her suffering. Instead, she allowed this long period of waiting to soften her heart toward God and to remind her who was the giver of life.

> *And she made a vow, saying, "Lord Almighty, if you will only look on your servant's misery and remember me, and not forget your servant but give her a son, then I will give him to the Lord for all the days of his life."* (1 Sam. 1:11)

Hannah not only prayed. She poured out her soul (verse 16). The priest, Eli, thought she was drunk. But Hannah hadn't been drinking. She was going to her secret place with the Lord, allowing him to see a place in her heart she hadn't revealed to anyone else.

Instead of assuming that her years of barrenness meant God had closed the door of her womb, Hannah made a bold request to the Lord. With a faith made bold through years of waiting, she went to him with the deepest desire of her heart, and God honored her.

What if we viewed waiting as a space for us to seek God's heart more? Rather than assume God has closed a door, what if we saw it as a chance to go to a place of deeper intimacy with him?

Instead of allowing her waiting period to become a distraction, Hannah chose to go deeper. The wait became a path to intimacy and turned into a legacy of faith that would be passed on for generations to come. Our wait can have the same result. When we see it as an opportunity instead of a roadblock, lives change, and miracles happen.

Back to that email. When I saw the hiring manager's response in my inbox, God showed me he was still working in the midst of the wait. As I followed the next steps outlined in the correspondence, I sensed him saying, "Keep pursuing this until I tell you to stop. Keep moving forward until the door is clearly shut."

And this is what I did. I don't want to assume God has closed a door because I lack persistence or follow-through. I want to keep knocking, keep waiting in faith and hope, and move forward when he says go.

The Training Ground for Righteousness

Even though my daughter made a turn in her fear of dogs after a month, our challenges with a new puppy weren't over. He ate anything he could fit in his mouth (and some things he couldn't). Anything within his reach was fair game. This included toys, any food left unattended, furniture, you name it. Multicolored poop filled our yard for months, and it looked like the Easter bunny decided to come for a random visit in late fall.

Habits like these caused his previous owners to say, "No thanks." But we were determined. While there were plenty of days when my patience wore thin, I knew that with time, attention, and plenty of discipline, he would be the perfect family dog.

These challenges with our new dog don't compare to other more difficult seasons our family has navigated together, but they reminded me how often we give up too soon. The road gets tough and we think, "God must not want me to pursue this route. Let's look for one that's easier." Or perhaps we stick with it for a season or two, but we're not seeing the results we anticipated. The dog takes longer to train than we want. Or the job search doesn't turn up the career for which we know God created us. So we say, "God is closing this door. I'll wait for him to open another one."

Yes, God does close doors. Often, we try to beat down doors he never wanted us to walk through in the first place. But there is a difference between a closed door and a distraction. Sometimes, God uses what appears to be a closed door as a training ground for righteousness. He uses it as an opportunity to shape our desires into his desires and to grow our character.

During these seasons, we remember the value of perseverance and patience. Our roots dig down into the soil God tills with his love, and we learn to resist the weather and the elements.

I don't use the word *perfect* very often, but Baxter is the perfect family dog. Yes, he needed lots of time and attention. But now I know he was the missing piece our family had been searching for. The time and the work could've been a distraction. In all honesty, they were at times. But in my mind, I could see the potential. I could see the future we hadn't yet witnessed.

Friend, as you examine the doors around you that you've written off as closed, I encourage you to do the same. Ask the Lord, who gives wisdom to those who ask, "Is this a closed door or a distraction?" If you're still unsure, use the test and approve method and sit unrushed in his presence.

If the door is closed, God will make it obvious. He is not a God of confusion or a God of what-ifs. But if it isn't, keep knocking, waiting, and persevering.

DISCUSSION QUESTIONS

1. Are there any areas of your life where you think God has closed a door but the "closed door" may just be a distraction? What do you think it would look like for you to move forward? Commit to praying about it, and notice how God shifts your perspective in the coming weeks.

2. Read 1 Samuel 1:11. Hannah could've perceived that God was permanently closing the door to her having a child; but instead, she persisted in prayer. What does Hannah's prayer reveal about her character? What can we learn from her patient persistence?

3. Has God ever used an obstacle in your life to grow your faith and perseverance? As you look back on that season of your life, what is one lesson you would pass on to others who are going through a similar struggle?

PART THREE

YOUR PLACE WITH HIM IS SECURE

"No one will snatch them out of my hand."

John 10:28

9

the hidden beauty of every misstep

I wanted to hide. My art teacher was going over our latest assignment, and each student's work was displayed across the wall for critique. This assignment was as simple as it was hard: paint a gray scale, starting with white and ending with black. Each shade of gray in between was supposed to be equal in its movement toward black. Mine was not, and it showed.

"Well, there's one that's too light and it sticks out like a sore thumb," the professor quipped.

As much as I tried to keep my facial expression neutral, I felt my face turning red.

Months before, when I had signed up for this college art class, I envisioned something therapeutic and fun. I needed a fine art for my major, and in my mind, I pictured everyone throwing some paint on a canvas without much care for rules. After all, I'd seen Jackson Pollock's work in my art history class. Wasn't he a renowned artist? After looking at the possible options for fulfilling the credit, I thought this one would be simple enough. But now we were two months in, and I realized this was not a sip-and-paint art class. It was difficult, and with each assignment, I became more discouraged.

Have you ever noticed a similar pattern in your spiritual life? Lord knows I have. I'm not saying I envision things being easy, because they never are. But when I take a step of faith, I often have an idea of how things will go. I have expectations and hopes, and I want to carry out whatever role he's asked me to pursue with excellence. And yet, there have been times when I've stepped out in faith, confident God is leading me, but then my expectations are met by my limitations. Sometimes, I haven't planned for an issue that arises or I encounter an obstacle I have no idea how to navigate. Other times, I'm simply not as good at something as I hoped I would be. In these moments, it's tempting to think, "Maybe this isn't what God wanted for me. Perhaps this endeavor was a mistake." Or we may say something like, "I'm not any good at this job. God must have someone else for this assignment."

There have been seasons when I've missed out on an opportunity because I think there's such a thing as perfect progress. But friends, the more I rely on my faith more than my need to appear competent, the more I realize there's no such thing. Progress means not only moving forward but messing up and figuring out what works. I've never seen a parent teach a kid how to ride a bike and say, "Okay, no falling allowed! If you fall, we're done. Lesson over." That would be completely unrealistic and ridiculous. And yet for some reason, we often adopt this perfection mindset in our spiritual lives.

What would it look like for us to embrace a learning mindset instead of a perfection mindset? If we approached those situations where the reality falls short of our expectations and asked, "What did I learn from this?" how would it change us? I believe adopting this perspective would change not only our spiritual health but our mental and emotional health as well. I believe it would give us the confidence to say yes amid uncertainty and to move in Jesus's pasture with freedom instead of fear.

No First Place Trophies in Heaven

In 2006, the year I got married, I had a bit of an obsession with actor and comedian Will Ferrell. It was the year his movie *Talladega Nights: The Ballad of Ricky Bobby* was released, which tells the tale of a NASCAR driver who spends much of his life trying to win his dad's approval. Even though his dad abandoned the family when Ricky was a baby, Ricky had a brief encounter with him at age ten when his dad told him, "If you're not first, you're last!" From that point on, Ricky lives his life by this motto. When he later becomes a racecar driver as an adult, nothing but first place will do.

Like most of Will Ferrell's movies, this one was filled with plenty of irreverent humor and silliness, but I can't help but wonder how often we embrace a similar mindset. Most of us, if we're willing to admit it, are seeking approval from someone. This desire is what fuels the perfection mindset because we think if we achieve whatever "perfection" means to us, we'll gain the approval we think we're lacking. If you've reached the point in your spiritual life where you can say, "I only seek approval from God," imagine me patting you on your back and saying "Well done." But most of us haven't reached that point.

> Here's what I think makes our eternal Father proud—when we take a risk, stumble through the unmet expectations and difficulties, and keep going.

Some of us seek approval from our parents. Others seek approval from their boss or peers. Even though his dad has never been part of his life, Ricky spends much of his life trying to attain a standard he thinks will make his dad proud. Here's what I think makes our eternal Father proud—when we take a risk, stumble through the unmet expectations and difficulties, and keep going. When we decide we're not going to let a few missteps along the way keep us from pursuing the goals and dreams he's entrusted us with, I believe there is applause in heaven. Because what matters is not achieving some invisible standard of perfection or earning accolades, but pointing souls toward the only One who truly embodies perfection.

But sometimes, I think we miss out on what he's saying to us and teaching us because we're obsessed with results. Whether it's numbers, trophies, or simply getting that nod of approval, our focus is on the outcome we see rather than the Father we can't see. And because of this skewed focus, we miss out on his speaking into our souls: *I'm crazy about you. I'm so proud of you for taking that risk even when you didn't know how it would turn out. You can't see it now, but I'm watering those seeds you planted.*

I am a visual person, so when we talk about these big concepts, it always helps me to see something concrete. As we talk about a perfection mindset versus a growth mindset, here's what it might look like in day-to-day life.

Perfection Mindset	Growth Mindset
A perfect outcome is the only way to honor God.	When love for God leads, he can use any outcome to bring growth and draw others to him.
Mistakes and missteps will cause God to abandon me.	God's love and faithfulness are not dependent on my actions.
If I fail at this, God will never be able to use me again.	God can always use someone who is willing and open to receiving correction.

Much to the dismay of all the Ricky Bobbies out there, Jesus makes it clear that our idea of first place and last will be turned on its head in heaven. When the disciples argue about who will be greatest in heaven, Jesus shuts down the conversation.

> *The kings of the Gentiles lord it over them; and those who exercise authority over them call themselves Benefactors. But you are not to be like that. Instead, the greatest among you should be like the youngest, and the one who rules like the one who serves. For who is greater, the one who is at the table or the one who serves? Is it not the one who is at the table? But I am among you as one who serves. You are those who have stood by me in my trials. And I confer on you a kingdom, just as my Father conferred one on me, so that you may eat and drink at my table in my kingdom and sit on thrones, judging the twelve tribes of Israel.* (Luke 22:25–30)

But you are not to be like that. In other words, we're to embrace a posture of humility. And sometimes, this means not taking ourselves so seriously or thinking we're too good to fail. Because when we fail, we learn. We grow and we take note of what worked and what didn't. We make adjustments and tweak our approach. Friend, I am preaching to myself here.

Remember that art class I told you about? Even though I was discouraged for weeks, I made progress. After several assignments, I understood what my professor was looking for and I adjusted my techniques. He noticed my improvement and effort, and my grade reflected it. Now I'll be the first to admit, I didn't embrace the growth mindset until after my professor noticed my improvement. I was still beating myself up over my seeming inability to do anything right. But regardless of how or when, growth happened. I realized I had an opportunity to *enjoy* the class instead of needing to be perfect, and that made all the difference.

The moments when God speaks to me in the clearest, most recognizable way are when I'm in situations that humble me. When I realize I'm in a situation I can't navigate on my own and I know I need his help, he shows up and amazes me in ways only he can. And when he does, I know it's his power working through my limitations because of how incapable I am. I know it's him speaking and working because my knowledge and resources are spent. These are the situations where God does some of his most magnificent work because I've finally recognized the true source and the reason for it all—and it isn't me.

But having these encounters with God means surrendering my need for certainty. It means being willing to accept my insufficiency and willing to make mistakes. When I do, God meets me and fills the gaps where I fall short. And when he does, I experience his presence in fresh, new ways.

How Far Jesus Will Go

If there's anyone who shows us the hidden beauty of our missteps, it's Peter. His story could've ended after he denied Jesus three times and the rooster crowed. He probably thought it had. After all, when Jesus was resurrected and found him on the Sea of Galilee, Peter had returned to what he knew: fishing. A fisherman by trade, he'd gone back to something he was good at. Something he was familiar with. An occupation where people don't get murdered after healing the sick and bringing hope to the lost. But Jesus had other plans for Peter.

I love how Jesus appears to Peter in this scene—in a completely unassuming way. He knows where Peter will be. He knows he will be hungry after a long night of work. So the first thing Jesus does after the miraculous catch, where Peter recognizes Jesus, is to make him and the other fisherman a meal. He starts the fire, cooks the fish, and breaks bread with his friends. Jesus knows that the heart of his disciples' faith rests in their connection with him. It rests in a relationship built around simple, everyday actions like eating together.

After their meal, Jesus has the most important conversation with Peter that is recorded in Scripture, and it starts with a single question, "Simon son of John, do you love me more than these?" (John 21:15). Although what Jesus is referring to in this passage has been questioned by scholars, the general understanding is that he is referring to the other friends who were there. It is the same question he asks each of us today: *What do you love the most?* Peter responds, "Yes, Lord, you know that I love you." But the conversation doesn't end there. Jesus asks, "Do you love me?" a total of three times, reflecting the exact number of times Peter denied him. The third time, John notes that Peter was hurt. But friends, Jesus's ultimate goal here isn't to hurt Peter. It's to show him where he's broken.

Jesus goes to the same lengths to reinstate Peter as Peter went in denying him. But then he goes a step further. He addresses the deepest need Peter has, the need all of us have. The need for humility. As Peter's story progresses in Acts and he becomes the person Jesus called "the Rock," we see this is not the same Peter who boasted that while others would fall away, he would not (Matt. 26:33). He is not the same Peter who cut off Malchus's ear or rebuked Jesus for predicting his death (John 18:10; Matt. 16:22). He is a changed man—one who is certain of one thing, and it's not of his own competency or ability. It's not in what tomorrow will bring. He's certain of the all-complete, redeeming power of Jesus. Our humility before God will always reflect our level of connection with God. A heart deceived by self-sufficiency and pride cannot connect with God who gave up everything to become a servant. This is why Jesus knew this conversation with Peter was crucial. He loved Peter too much to let his purpose for him be thwarted.

Our humility before God will always reflect our level of connection with God.

If it hadn't been for Peter's missteps, this moment on the beach with Jesus would never have happened. But I'm so glad it did. Because within this treasure of a scene, we see where our certainty lies. It lies not in our ability to measure up or always get it right but in the all-sufficient love and sacrifice of Jesus. Once we realize this truth, I believe the Spirit communicates with us in new ways because our priorities are aligned with his.

Guarded by the One Who Defeated Death

Every spring, we hear them—coyotes. This time of year means cubbing season, and it's not unusual for them to roam into the outer perimeter of our yard. We live on about two acres of land, and although it's in a neighborhood, various types of wildlife make it their grazing area on a regular basis. Deer are the most common, but we've also seen wild turkeys, foxes, bears, and my least favorite—the coyotes. Although most of the other animals are harmless, we must be cautious of the coyotes, especially when our dog is outside. While Baxter is not a runner like my first pup, he loves to play with other dogs—even if they're wild.

Last year during cubbing season, my husband took Baxter outside and immediately saw the shadows around the edge of the yard. Then the yipping started. The playful sound said, "Come a little closer. We want to play." Baxter's tail started wagging and my husband had to tell him no in his firmest voice.

Thank God, Baxter listened. But I know this incident will not be the last.

It made me think of the passage we've been studying in John 10. The thieves and robbers are always there, trying to infiltrate the pasture. And as long as we're living, they'll continue. If my husband, who is a flawed human being with a sinful nature, protects our dog from wild coyotes looking for a quick meal, how much more will Jesus protect us? His protection isn't conditional. It is eternal. Once we decide to enter the pasture, his protection never stops.

But sometimes, the Enemy convinces us it will. This is one of his greatest deceptions. If he can convince us that Jesus's protection will end, he can convince us that the blood failed. Instead of our tomorrow being secure in Jesus, its security now rests in something else. Our successes and failures. Our highs and lows. But this mindset couldn't be further from the truth. In his book *Praying Like Monks, Living Like Fools*, Tyler Staton explains how our mistakes and weaknesses are the means God can use to draw us into his presence if we let him. However, our reaction to his grace and mercy is often to do the opposite.

> *Our intuitive assumption is that we are closest to God when things are going well. Jesus is by my side, present and helping, when I'm living wisely and virtuously, keeping in step with his mission in me and in the world. The author of Hebrews says the exact opposite. Jesus is nearest to us in "our weaknesses," not our strengths. Our hearts, corrupted by sin, are like the poles of a magnet that push away, ever resistant to grace.*[1]

In the verse Staton refers to here, the author of Hebrews tells us to come *boldly* to the throne of grace. Not with our tail between our legs or with our face downcast. We're to come with confidence. Why? Because Jesus understands.

> *This High Priest of ours understands our weaknesses, for he faced all of the same testings we do, yet he did not sin. So let us come boldly to the throne of our gracious God. There we will receive his mercy, and we will find grace to help us when we need it most.* (Heb. 4:15–16 NLT)

When was the last time we came to God boldly after we failed? While I'm getting better at coming to him in my need, I wouldn't call my prayers bold. Meek or reluctant would be a better word. But *bold* is the exact posture the writer of Hebrews tells us to take. Other translations say "with confidence." Friends, this is not a daughter or a son who is worried about her Dad kicking her out of the pasture. This is a child who knows her Father will leave the other ninety-nine to come after her, and nothing she can say or do will stop him from loving her.

But we can't expect to discern God's voice and his leading in our lives if we're unwilling to come to him when we're weak. We can't expect closeness if we keep pushing him away. However, if we come to him and admit our mess-ups, our need, and our shortcomings, he meets us there. It's there, when we put aside our pride and self-sufficiency, that we often hear him the loudest and the most clearly.

The God Who Prays for Us

Before Simon Peter ever hears the rooster crow, Jesus shows how much he loves him. First, he predicts Simon's betrayal and prepares him for what's to come. Then, in a simple statement, he reveals that he's already petitioning for Simon, giving him the best gift aside from his own death: He's praying for him. "Simon,

Simon, Satan has asked to sift each of you like wheat. But I have pleaded in prayer for you, Simon, that your faith should not fail" (Luke 22:31–32 NLT). Jesus was making a way for Peter to come home before he even knew he needed to.

Friend, do you know he's praying for you too? In one of the most beautiful prayers recorded in Scripture, he prays for every believer who will come to know him.

> *My prayer is not for them alone. I pray also for those who will believe in me through their message, that all of them may be one, Father, just as you are in me and I am in you. May they also be in us so that the world may believe that you have sent me.* (John 17:20–21)

To be one with him means to let him invade every part of our lives, even the ones we want to hide or skip over. Our honesty and humility are the pathway to wholeness. He sees not only the ways you'll fail and falter but the person you'll become on the other side. He sees your heart and knows your deepest fears. When he said, "No one will snatch them out of my Father's hand," he meant it.

DISCUSSION QUESTIONS

1. In this chapter, we talked about the difference between a perfection mindset and a growth mindset. Has there ever been a time when a perfection mindset kept you from moving forward? What do you think it would look like for you to embrace a growth mindset instead?

2. Read John 21:15–19. Why do you think Jesus asks Peter if he loves him three times? What do you think the key message of this passage is?

3. Has there ever been a time in your life when failure caused you to grow in your faith? What did you learn about God through your experience?

10

the danger of too many opinions

Several months ago, I logged onto Facebook and read a post from someone asking when she should put up her Christmas tree. Now, I've been guilty of similar posts myself, but a few friends echoed my thoughts in their response to her question: "You're an adult. Put it up when you feel like it." I can't help but wonder how this lack of confidence in our choices affects our spiritual lives as well.

If you're anything like me, you sometimes come to God expecting immediate guidance in major decisions or life changes, but then realize God isn't on our timeline. Our sense of his direction comes from the time we've invested in getting to know him. It comes from the moments we've spent seeking him when there *isn't* a life-altering choice to be made or a decision we need to make right now.

About ten years ago, Pandora Jewelry released a commercial that ended up going viral on social media and was shared on news stations nationwide.[1] The commercial showed six young children, around eight years old and younger, being blindfolded in a large room as their moms stood on the other side. One by one, they were spun around and released. Then each of them walked across the room in search of their mother. Using mostly the sense of touch, each child found his or her mom without fail.

What was the magic behind these kids' sense of knowing? Time spent with their moms. They didn't need to be able to see them. They knew their mom's unique touch and smell. They remembered the texture of their mom's hair and the way her stomach felt as they pressed their faces against it.

As I thought about this commercial, I wondered whether these six kids would've found their moms if the room had been filled with thousands of other people shouting their names. If they'd been spun around, blindfolded, and released into a room filled with chaos, would they have been as successful? Probably not. The noise would've been too distracting, and even though they weren't relying on their sense of sound, each kid sought his or her mom with intention and with other senses engaged.

Too often, I think we take this approach with God. We expect to be able to engage with him and hear from him while distracted by thousands of other voices at the same time. Lord knows I've been guilty. We live in an age where it has never been easier to find knowledge on a particular topic and seek opinions from complete strangers. There is a guru for everything under the sun, including spiritual direction and discernment. But what happens when these other voices create dissonance, affecting our ability to discern God's voice? With thousands of directions and opinions at our fingertips, where does God come in? What if there's a line we need to draw when it comes to seeking guidance from other people?

This distinction applies not only to social media and the internet but to our real-life, day-to-day relationships as well. A few years ago, I began my coaching business for writers, and I realized how perplexing it can be when you receive conflicting information from people who are trying to help you. I coached a few clients who were meeting with other coaches as well, although these other coaches specialized in different areas. Nonetheless, whenever I gave clients guidance that seemed to contradict what they'd been told by someone else, they were confused and sometimes frustrated. And I couldn't blame them. Often, these varying opinions keep us in a state of inertia, asking the perpetual question, "Which way should I go?" We want clarity, but the Information Age can leave us with the exact opposite, leading to more questions than answers.

Seeking God before Seeking Others

If I look back at my history with God and the times I've sought direction for big decisions, one thing is consistent. The times when I've felt the most peace and clarity are when I didn't go to others first. This realization has led me to seek him first in those moments rather than the opinions of others. The one exception to this would be when the decision involves my husband; but even then, he is usually not the first person I go to. I spend days, often weeks in prayer before consulting others. Why? Because I don't want his voice and his nudges to become convoluted in the voices of others. When I humble myself before God and wait for his leading, he honors it.

Here's another hard truth I've realized about God's leading. When I go to others, it's often because the road of following God has gotten hard. I want an out or an excuse to give up. My pride leads me to believe I need to move past whatever hurdle or dilemma I'm facing right now, and I'm not willing to go through the honest seeking, waiting, and listening of refinement. But friends, the refining is always worth it.

David is a remarkable example of how seeking God first leads us not only to clarity but to victory. As I studied the Old Testament this year, I noticed a continual habit he practiced. Whenever he went into battle, he sought the Lord first and asked whether or not he should proceed. Not his military leaders or the priests. Not his family. He went to *God himself* and asked for guidance. And each time he did this, God handed his enemies over to him.

> *Then David inquired of the LORD: "Should I attack the Philistines? Will you hand them over to me?"*
>
> *The LORD replied to David, "Attack, for I will certainly hand the Philistines over to you."*
>
> *So David went to Baal-perazim and defeated them there and said, "Like a bursting flood, the LORD has burst out against my enemies before me." Therefore, he named that place The Lord Bursts Out.* (2 Sam. 5:19–20 CSB)

Now here's one truth we need to be clear on. David was able to hear God in these moments because of the time he spent fostering this relationship in the past. This wasn't a once-in-a-while, come-to-him-when-I-need-him encounter with God. David had spent time with God in the wilderness, seeking him, writing psalms, and praying to him as he was pursued by King Saul. He wrestled with God and shared his emotions with him when he felt alone and discouraged. Time spent with God enabled him to hear the voice of God.

Friends, going to God first is not part of a live-your-truth, do-what-feels-good-to-you gospel. In fact, it is the exact opposite. It's a commitment to abide in the One who knows. It's a commitment to listen to his voice, even when we're afraid we'll get it wrong. Which brings me to another reason why we often go to others before going to God: We're afraid we'll falter or mishear him.

Safe with the True Shepherd

In the final promise from John 10 that we will explore together, Jesus makes another bold statement. Like the other truths Jesus shares here, it is short but packed with beauty and reassurance. He says of his sheep, "I give them eternal life, and they shall never perish; no one will snatch them out of my hand" (John 10:28).

Throughout this passage, the emphasis is not on the sheep's abilities but on Jesus's sacrificial care. Jesus highlights only one ability—their ability to hear him. Why? Because this is the only ability needed. Everything else is not up to us but dependent on the One who gave his life. The security of the sheep rests not on their capabilities but on the Shepherd.

> Jesus highlights only one ability—their ability to hear him. Why? Because this is the only ability needed.

As I thought of these comforting words from Jesus, I thought of my first dog. She was my first "baby" and the reason my husband and I met, but that is another story for another book. She was a cute rottweiler mix, a ball of mischief, and a loyal dog. But she was also a runner. Unlike the sheep in this passage, she followed no one but her nose.

There were hundreds of things that beckoned our mutt to the woods covering the mountaintop we called home for ten years, and most of them ran on four legs too. She smelled their scents, followed their trails, and despite the comfort of a warm house and a full bowl of food, she was on the move before I could give my best whistle. On more than one occasion, I thought she was gone for good. Visions of wild animals that called this mountain their home filled my head, and I was certain my runner had met her match.

On one particular occasion when she was old and a bit senile, she was gone for longer than usual. I posted a call for help on Facebook, along with her picture. I called the local shelters with no success, and my mind turned to the worst-case scenario. I felt like the worst dog mom ever. Then, after a couple of days, a watchful neighbor returned her to our doorstep. I collapsed onto her chilled, tail-wagging frame. I wanted to chide her and rebuke her for the worry and sleeplessness she'd caused, but all I could do was hug her and run my hands through her soft fur.

It wasn't the rebuke that kept her home all those years. It was the kindness.

And you know what? The love I had for this wayward dog doesn't even begin to encompass the love I have for my kids. And yet, there have been many times in my life when I thought God would abandon me for misinterpreting his leading, misstepping, or faltering. Even when my intentions were led by my love for him. Even when I sought him and prayed for his guidance.

Because of this fear, I've looked for an affirming word or guidance from others when God had already given me direction. I want to know for sure that it's his voice I'm hearing and to discern whether the path I'm considering will lead me astray. But friends, unless I'm about to do something that explicitly contradicts God's Word, can someone else perceive what God spoke to my heart? I realize this is a loaded question, but it's worth considering. As I've studied Scripture, here's what I've realized: Unless the Holy Spirit revealed his prompting to someone else, the answer is no.

Can God still use others to affirm his Word? Absolutely, and he does. In fact, a word from the Lord can come from the most unexpected places. We see a striking example of this truth in

Acts 10. Peter has a strange vision while praying on a rooftop and doesn't know what it means. In his vision, animals of all kinds are lowered from heaven on a large sheet, and Peter is instructed to "kill and eat" (Acts 10:13). According to Old Testament law, these animals are unclean, and Peter will not hear of committing this violation of his Jewish custom. But God always has a reason for speaking to us, and he will not leave us alone to fumble through the dark. Whom does God use to help Peter interpret this vision? A Gentile centurion named Cornelius. The same Spirit who inspires Peter's vision appears to this man and gives clear, specific instructions to send for Peter. Because Peter is open to the Spirit's leading, an entire household of Gentiles is saved and baptized in the Holy Spirit. For the first time, Peter sees God's bigger plan: He did not come to save only the Jews but everyone who will receive Jesus as Lord.

God can use anyone he desires to speak to us. Whether it's a complete stranger, a family member, or a friend, these people can give us the reassurance we need to move forward. Friends, this is a beautiful thing. We need these people in our lives. We need community to remind us what we're capable of when we follow Christ and to speak life into us when we're filled with doubt and fear. God used an unlikely person whom Peter saw as an outsider to help him interpret his vision, and because of this man's obedience, lives were changed. But other times, the opinions of others can cause us to question God, hesitate, and take a completely different path. Even believers are flawed humans, and sometimes our desire for security leads us more than a desire to follow Jesus.

When Our Search Leads Us Back to Ourselves

Over the past few years as I've sought God's direction for my life and wisdom concerning decisions, he's shown me that the way forward is often more obvious than I think. Sometimes I seek the guidance and wisdom of others in spaces where he's already given clear instruction or stated his will in his Word. Here are three areas where we may seek others' counsel for truths God has already confirmed.

We look to others to tell us who we are. Only God can tell us who we are. His identity and stamp of approval stick, while others will ebb and flow with the tide. But we seek others' opinions, words, and personality tests to tell us who we are all the time, don't we? You can see this truth with the popularity of the Enneagram and the massive number of books published on this topic. Now, I am a huge fan of personality tests and in case you are interested, I am a six on the Enneagram. These tests pull me in and fascinate my need to understand my unique disposition. And while none of these tools are wrong in and of themselves, they can become dangerous to our growth when we allow them to replace the identity given to us by God alone. Others can affirm what he's already said or determined, but they can't replace it or take it away. Take, for example, our gifts.

In Chapter Three, we talked about kids and how they don't feel fear in pursuing or talking about the things they love. They haven't become jaded by the world or told their dreams are unrealistic, and their creativity seems as though it has no bounds. They are free, and they use the gifts God has given them without shame. But somewhere in the journey of life, this carefree nature changes. Whether it's because of a callous comment from a teacher or peer or rejection, we don't see this level of creative freedom in adulthood.

Often, in our longing for approval or our innate need to be defined by someone or something, we look to others to affirm the gifts God already gave us at birth. We want someone to tell us, "You're an artist," or "You're a really gifted speaker." When we don't receive this affirmation, we may assume we never had those gifts to begin with. As a result, we pursue a path completely different from the one God prepared in advance for us to walk in (Eph. 2:10).

In his book *The Soul of Shame*, Curt Thompson discusses this loss of creative spirit and gifts, stressing that it isn't something we should ignore. It is a birthright given to us by God, and when we don't make an active effort to recover it, we deny ourselves purpose and meaning.

> *Shame is a primary means to prevent us from using gifts we have been given. And those gifts enable us to flourish as a light-bearing community of Jesus followers who work to create space for others who wish to join it to do so. Shame, therefore, is not simply an unfortunate, random, emotional event that came with us out of the primordial evolutionary soup. It is both a source and result of evil's active assault on God's creation, and a way for evil to try to hold out until the new heaven and earth appear at the consummation of history.*[2]

As Thompson further explains, kids crave security. For the early parts of their lives, this security comes primarily from their parents. In a healthy home, the child feels safe, creativity is nurtured, and the child continues to grow. But once this security is damaged, it must be repaired or healed.

I know Thompson's words to be true because for a decade after I graduated from college, I placed my gift of being a communicator on the back burner. When I sought counsel from my college adviser, he told me I needed a higher GPA to pursue a career in editing and suggested I pursue other paths. Since I didn't think a writing job would prove lucrative, I got a desk job working at an insurance company and didn't think much about writing until after the birth of my first child. This job checked off the boxes of security and certainty; and even though I wasn't using my gifts, the risk factor was low. To be honest, this job I held in my early twenties could probably be filled by AI in today's world. It was mindless and robotic. There was no creativity involved.

While I don't fault my adviser and believe he told me what he'd seen firsthand, I also know his words contributed to the narrative I played in my head. And the narratives we listen to matter. They affect the trajectory of our lives and can cause us to bury the gifts God has given us to use for his glory. Will he chase after us? Absolutely! But often, we are oblivious to him when he nudges us toward a different route.

One of the ways God speaks to and guides his children is through their unique gifts and talents. While some are developed over time, others are ingrained into our DNA. This is why it's important for us to never let the other voices in our lives become louder than God's. Others may not see the distinct gifts he placed within us, but he does. When we walk away from these gifts, we miss opportunities for God to guide us.

We look to others to affirm a promise God has given or a word he has spoken to us. While God may use others to affirm what he's said and give us confidence on the path ahead, we will become frustrated if we always seek other flawed humans to become interpreters for God. He guides us and speaks to each of us in unique ways, and my way of discerning his guidance may be different from someone else's.

Now, I want to be clear here on one key truth. God will never speak to us or guide us in a way that contradicts his Word.

This is why it's important for us to know Scripture, and for us to establish a regular rhythm of immersing ourselves in it. Without it, we will not know whether it is God's voice we are hearing or not. His Word is an integral part of his communication with us and through us.

God's Word is our first line of defense against being misled by our flawed perception. But when we turn to others to confirm a word from the Lord, we need to be on our guard as well. Because as we've stated, many times they won't. As we can see in Scripture, sometimes our need for confirmation from others will lead us in the opposite direction than the one God wants for us. We see this in Numbers when Moses sends spies to scout the land God promised to give the Israelites.

God had declared his promise to deliver the nation of Israel into the land of Canaan throughout the book of Exodus. It is like a repeated stanza throughout its chapters, reminding a forgetful people that he does not forget his Word. Every time the Israelites encounter an obstacle or complain, he performs miracles and provides for their needs through Moses and Aaron. At this point, you would think they've had sufficient evidence to see who God is and to know whether or not they can trust him. And yet, when one group decides not to listen to Joshua and Caleb's report of a land ready to be taken and flowing with milk and honey, thousands of other Israelites are led astray. Instead of trusting the word God gave them and walking into their promised future, they reject it. They forfeit the blessing, both for themselves and their children.

Their words in Numbers 14 reveal how far their hearts have been misled.

> *Then the whole community broke into loud cries,*
> *and the people wept that night. All the Israelites*

> *complained about Moses and Aaron, and the whole community told them, "If only we had died in the land of Egypt, or if only we had died in this wilderness! Why is the* Lord *bringing us into this land to die by the sword? Our wives and children will become plunder. Wouldn't it be better for us to go back to Egypt?" So they said to one another, "Let's appoint a leader and go back to Egypt."* (Num. 14:1–4 CSB)

Not only do the Israelites listen to a message contradictory to what God told them, but they accuse God of leading them into the promised land to be killed and plundered. Their words create a picture of a heartless God who says one thing and does another while luring his people to their deaths. Can you see why God is angry?

Because of the Israelites' distrust, many of them never saw the promised land. This heartbreaking chapter in their story shows the importance of trusting God at his word and being mindful of second opinions. And when we do seek another opinion, we need to be sure that we go to someone who displays trust in the Lord, who believes he will do what he says he will do even when others say otherwise.

We look to others to tell us our purpose. I spent most of my twenties looking for someone to tell me my purpose. I wasn't seeking God's Word or his direction for my life, and I listened to many people give false versions of what my true purpose was. My purpose was to find true happiness. My purpose was to do good and live a good life. None of these narratives brought fulfillment, and after years of searching, God placed a few people in my life who pointed me toward him. I realized he was my reason for living, breathing, and creating.

We don't need others to tell us our purpose, because God's Word tells us what it is. Our reason for being on this planet is to glorify him, point others to him, and bring others with us into the kingdom of heaven. But how we live this out will look different depending on our unique gifts, talents, and experiences. My way of communicating the love of God will not look the same as someone whose favorite pastime is running track or coaching athletics. Those strengths aren't in my wheelhouse, but those people will be able to reach others I cannot.

Do you know who else never let others tell him his purpose? Jesus. There were plenty of people who tried, but Jesus knew his purpose could be defined by only One, his Father in heaven. Even though he told his disciples he would die, they didn't understand. Peter went so far as to rebuke Jesus for saying this after he had just declared Jesus as the Messiah. But Jesus knew why he had come and was having none of it.

> *Jesus turned and said to Peter, "Get behind me, Satan! You are a stumbling block to me; you do not have in mind the concerns of God, but merely human concerns."* (Matt. 16:23)

While Jesus's words may seem harsh, he knew the suffering and the testing that lay ahead of him. Even *he* would wrestle and question on the final night in Gethsemane before his crucifixion. But he also knew if he was going to carry out his purpose without being thwarted by the will of others, he had to be single-minded in his focus. Others may not have understood why he came, but he did.

When Others Need to Get behind You

While I don't recommend saying "Get behind me, Satan" to your friends and family members, Jesus's response to Peter is a good example of how we should respond to those who thwart our purpose. Paul gives us another good example in Galatians 2. When Peter seemingly forgets what the Spirit revealed to him about the Gentiles and imposes Jewish law on them, Paul rebukes him. Paul reminds him of God's purpose to redeem both the Jews and the Gentiles and will not stand by while someone distracts from this truth (Gal. 2:11–16).

Friend, the best way to remember our purpose is to stay rooted in Jesus. Now, some of you might say, "I know my purpose, but I don't know what my gifts are." This would be an instance where I ask you, "What keeps you up at night? What lights a fire in your spirit and makes you say, 'Someone really needs to do something about that'?" When we pay attention to these moments, they often point us toward our passions. When we know what our passions are, this knowledge often leads us to discover our gifts and strengths. Sometimes, if we're surrounded by a healthy church body or community, others can see abilities in us that we can't. When you ask others what your strengths are, what do they say? Is there something your friends and community consistently praise? If so, pay attention because God often uses these people as arrows toward our next steps.

Because we live in a post-Eden world, this is not always the case. There will be times when people won't understand what God has asked us to do. They'll voice their opinions, point out the risks, and sometimes try to deter us. In those scenarios, remember the words of Jesus. Voice them to yourself, to your spirit who knows the Shepherd who leads you. He won't lead you astray, friend. And no one, not a single soul, will snatch you out of his hand.

DISCUSSION QUESTIONS

1. Have the voices of others, whether in person or online, ever made it difficult to discern the voice of God? What did you do in response to this problem? Or, if you didn't do anything, what actions can you take in the future?

2. Read Numbers 14:1–4. Even though God had repeated his promise to be with the Israelites and deliver the promised land into their hands, we see them listen to a voice that completely contradicts this promise. Why do you think it was so easy for the Israelites to believe a lie that contradicted God's words? What is one thing you can do to help you recognize lies from others?

3. In this chapter we discussed the final promise from John 10: "I give them eternal life, and they shall never perish; no one will snatch them out of my hand" (John 10:28). How does this verse provide reassurance as you continue the journey of listening to God's voice and acting on it? If you kept this verse at the forefront of your mind when facing the unknown, how do you think it would change your perspective?

11

the person you are now is not the person you're becoming

A garden was not anywhere on my radar for "fun" summer activities. For one, my record of keeping plants alive is not stellar. And two, the animals I mentioned in the previous chapter have a habit of turning anything I plant into their personal salad bar. But when my two younger kids attended vacation Bible school and farm life was the theme, I knew what was coming. Sure enough, on the last day, they brought home an egg carton filled with assorted vegetable seedlings. Before I knew it, we were growing tiny beans, tomatoes, and peppers in our backyard. Who was this person in the mirror? I didn't even recognize her. But then something even more unexpected happened.

Each time I went outside and checked on our little raised garden, I felt a surge of excitement. A sense of gratitude and accomplishment. I'd heard friends talk about the rewards and the spiritual benefits of gardening, but now I understood it.

Something we'd planted, nurtured, and cared for was growing right in front of us, with each day birthing new signs of health and life. From tiny buds to flowering plants to produce, we saw each stage of the cycle.

Now trust me, I will not be holding out for the Food Network to contact me about starting my own home gardening show, but the experience reminded me how God loves to birth something new in us. He loves to take an endeavor we didn't even know we would enjoy or be capable of doing and say, "See? I'm making a stream where you saw nothing. I'm creating beauty where you only saw past failures."

But we don't always see the same tangible evidence of growth with our faith, do we? Sometimes we get discouraged because we pour out our time, efforts, and resources into our families, communities, and churches but feel like we have little to show for it.

Other times, we adopt the same attitude I did when I realized a garden was in my future—we're reluctant. We may not even take the step of faith because we only see the person we are now. The person who failed at all previous attempts to change her situation. The person who tried something new, but it didn't go the way she anticipated. We make decisions based on what we know—our gifts, talents, and past accomplishments. But you know what? God sees someone else. He sees not only the person you are now but the new creation he's birthing within. Not only that, but he sees the parts of our story we can't yet see and the work he will do through us.

Peter, whose story we've been exploring, is a perfect example of this truth. Jesus knew Peter would deny him three times, but he also knew that wasn't the end of his story. He saw the narrative on the other side of Peter's failure and the man he would become. This is why in Jesus's interaction with Peter at the Last

Supper, we don't see him question whether Peter will return. Remember how Jesus said he would pray for him? Right after he says this, he makes a confident statement about Peter's future.

> *So* ***when*** *you have repented and turned to me again, strengthen your brothers.* (Luke 22:32 NLT—emphasis added)

Although Peter responds, "Lord, I am ready to go to prison with you, and even to die with you," Jesus knew he was not yet ready to make this claim. But he would be. On the other side of his pride, denial, grief, and questioning, Peter would be a changed man. Jesus recognized that who Peter was as a person was not stagnant. And the same is true for you and me.

I wonder how often we miss opportunities God gives us because we're more desperate to hold on to who we are than to experience who we're becoming. Sticking with what we know feels safe and secure. We feel certain of our competency in specific areas, and the possibility of trying something new seems risky at best, and foolish at worst. But what if God reveals a beautiful facet of the person we're becoming on the other side of our shaky yes?

> I wonder how often we miss opportunities God gives us because we're more desperate to hold on to who we are than to experience who we're becoming.

Loving Enough to Lead

My middle child, Gabe, didn't think he was a musician. In his mind, that talent was reserved for his big brother, who plays piano and violin. When he reached his fourth-grade year and the band was offered as an extracurricular activity, I asked him whether he planned to join.

"No, I'll try it next year."

I had a feeling this was a stalling tactic, but I let it slide the first year. Sure enough, he told me the exact same thing in fifth grade when the option to join the band was given. But this time, I wasn't falling for it. During this season of parenting, God kept pressing one encouragement on my heart: *Trust your instincts.*

"Gabe, you're going to try the band for one year," I said. "If you don't like it, you can quit next year."

Surprisingly, he didn't try to argue. After the band teacher came into the school and did a presentation on various instruments, Gabe picked the trombone. They had practice a couple times a week, and he was allowed to use a trombone owned by the school system while he decided whether it was something he wanted to stick with in future years.

About a month after band started in the fall, Gabe came up to me one evening and said, "Mom, I really like playing trombone. Mrs. Johnson tells me I'm a good player." I smiled and told him how happy I was for him. Later in the year, I got to hear him and the other members play for the first time. I witnessed the joy on his face and his eagerness to display his abilities for the rest of the school.

I'm so grateful I pushed my son to try something new and trusted God's prompting. I gave him the same encouragement God had given me in recent ministry and business endeavors: You won't know if you don't try. And since both of his parents were former members of their high school marching bands, I had a gut feeling he would love it. I knew Gabe was still discovering his unique gifts, strengths, and passions. Who he is as a person is not static—he's still growing and developing. And you know what? The same is true for us.

But I will also be the first to tell you that there have been times when I've given in to the excuses or not trusted God's prompting. Whether I'm just tired and don't want to argue, or afraid I'll be wrong, I decide not to push the issue. Other times, I've pushed my kids to do things they didn't enjoy because I saw all the other moms signing their kids up, and the fear of missing out took over. Instead of paying attention to the nudges and the instincts God gave me as a mom, I followed what everyone else was doing. Parenting is a constant ebb and flow of finding what makes our kids light up, learning how God made them, and encouraging them to push through their fears. We won't always get it right. But goodness, we crave some sort of affirmation when we do get it right, don't we?

If there was ever an area where we crave certainty, it's in raising our kids. We want God to give us a giant sign with an arrow saying, "This is the way! Walk in it." The pressure of the constant presence of social media is overwhelming. There seems to be an underlying fear that if we don't get our kids signed up for every activity under the sun when they're four, they'll miss out on a major scholarship or a chance to play in a professional league. We want to know we're guiding them in the right way and see them grow up to be thriving adults. We want them to love Jesus, make good decisions, and know that the temporary things of this world will never satisfy. But at the same time we want to control outcomes and push them toward the path of life, we also realize we have to let them go. We must release them to the One who surrendered his own Son and trust that he loves them more than we ever could.

While their personalities, likes, and dislikes give me clues, I don't know who my kids will become. But God does. And the more I relinquish my grip and trust him with their futures, the more I see the certainties I do have. I am certain of my constant love for them and my devotedness to teaching them about their Savior. I am certain of God's unwavering love for them. Because I know these things, I can surrender my need for certainty about the rest. Is it easy? Not one bit. But when I do, his peace covers me.

As I walk through all these seasons of parenting and growth in my kids, God shows that he's birthing new things in me too. But to see this newness flourish, I must be willing to move with him.

Willing to Be Transformed

Several years ago, I went through a season in my spiritual life where I felt stuck. Now, it wasn't the first time this had happened, and I'm sure it won't be the last, but this time was different. My tried-and-true ways of connecting with God weren't working and discouragement weighed on me like a constant shadow. It seemed like no matter how much Scripture I consumed or how much I prayed, I wasn't connecting with God the way I used to.

For months, I'd felt prompted to take a huge step with my online ministry, but I didn't think I was qualified. While I believed God was leading me to expand my services, I reasoned that I needed further training and that the technical challenges were too complicated. Because of my constant reasoning and doubting, an internal restlessness grew. And the more I journey with God, the more I realize this type of restlessness usually indicates something needs to change. Let's go back to our key passage in John 10 to find clues about what this change looks like.

When Jesus tells the Pharisees, "No one will snatch them out of my Father's hand" in John 10, he is speaking of life and freedom to a group of people bound by their own self-made rules. He took their limiting constructs about who the Messiah was and turned them upside down. But we often bind ourselves by limiting God too, don't we? We talk ourselves out of good things

God wants us to pursue before we even get started because we can't see the person he sees. We don't see the leader we'll become if we can just move past our "I'm not leadership material" mentality. We don't see the speaker we'll become if we can move past the fact that our first few talks will be bad.

> We talk ourselves out of good things God wants us to pursue before we even get started because we can't see the person he sees.

Paul has a lot to say about freedom and transformation in the New Testament. We talked about this passage from 2 Corinthians briefly in Chapter Four, but here I want to study how it addresses our growth:

> *Now the Lord is the Spirit, and where the Spirit of the Lord is, there is freedom. And we all, who with unveiled faces contemplate the Lord's glory, are being transformed into his image with ever-increasing glory, which comes from the Lord, who is the Spirit.* (2 Cor. 3:17–18)

Let's focus on the word "transformed" here for a moment. It means that who we are isn't stationary. But we can't be transformed if we're clutching tightly to the person we are now, afraid to try something out of the ordinary. While our identity as a child of God does not change, the ways we reflect his image do. The reflection of his glory becomes greater and greater as we move with him, leaving behind the person who was confined by doubt.

Now, I want to be clear about something here because there's a key to our transformation we often forget. Our transformation can never be achieved through our own striving, strength, or willpower. Trying to produce change in this way will only make us weary and disillusioned. It is only through the working of the Holy Spirit and our abiding in his presence that we will experience true, lasting change. This means being sensitive to his leading and responding to his prompts. Our renewal is not the result of our grand ideas or brilliance but his.

Moving with his Spirit may look like one of the following examples.

Confessing our limiting beliefs to God and allowing him to speak new life to our hearts. If our first thought when God prompts us to do something is "I can't," our next best step is to confess this limiting belief to him. The Holy Spirit wants to refine us but will not force his way into our lives. He will prompt us, lead us toward truth, and invite us, but our sensitivity to his leading requires an ongoing relationship. And just like any relationship, we can't be sensitive to the characteristics and eccentricities of someone we shut out of our lives. As Paul reminds us in Ephesians 4, the Holy Spirit is not some distant, mystical force but a personal being who cares for us.

> *Do not grieve the Holy Spirit of God, with whom you were sealed for the day of redemption.* (Eph. 4:30)

Can we pause for a moment here and marvel at the fact that the God of the universe grieves for us? His mind is affected by our actions and inaction. Someone who does not care for us would not experience grief when we practice unhealthy behavior. Only an intimate, compassionate God who desires what is best for us would.

Trying things we know only God can equip us to do. If we're only relying on our talent and experience, we'll have little opportunity to see God move. This doesn't mean we don't prepare and do our work with excellence, but it also means allowing space for God to intervene in ways only he can. In these moments, his power and his presence are undeniable, and lives are impacted.

I love Paul's reminder to the church at Corinth, "For the kingdom of God is not a matter of talk but of power" (1 Cor. 4:20). As someone who can think and talk through things until I'm blue in the face, it's a good reminder that God's power will be displayed when I *act.*

Doing something no one in our church or community has done before. I don't know about you, but it's much easier for me to be a follower. When someone else takes the lead and my job is simply to support their efforts, it feels less risky. And while there's certainly nothing wrong with serving ministries and communities others lead, sometimes God asks us to go where no one else has gone before us. He asks us to be the leader. These are the times when he births new abilities and passions in us, ones we may not see otherwise. In the words of Oswald Chambers, "Beware of harking back to what you once were when God wants you to be something you have never been."[1]

When I felt stuck in my spiritual life several years ago, I was finally honest with God about it. I don't know why it took me so long to tell him, because he already knew, but somehow my admission felt like whining. Although there wasn't a sudden change in my situation, my consistent conversations with him brought a realization: My inertia in my spiritual life reflected my inertia in my business and ministry life. When I took the step I knew God was leading me toward and let go of my excuses, I experienced new growth. I felt a joy I hadn't known in years and discovered talents I didn't even know I possessed.

Always under Construction

If there was ever a person who knew the power of renewal by the Spirit and displayed it in her life, it was Ruth Bell Graham. Many of my friends and family members have visited the Billy Graham Library, where you can learn about the legacy of Rev. Graham and his wife, Ruth. Their gravesites can also be visited there, and Ruth's epitaph reveals the heart of someone who knew her transformation in this life was an ongoing process.

Our Daily Bread talks about the words and the inspiration behind them:

> *Years ago, Ruth Bell Graham, wife of evangelist Billy Graham, saw a sign by the road: "End of Construction—Thank you for your patience." Smiling, she remarked that she wanted those words on her gravestone.*
>
> *After her death in June 2007, her desire was carried out. Her grave marker bears the Chinese character for* righteousness *(Mrs. Graham was born in China), followed by the words that made her smile.*[2]

For those who don't know Ruth's history, this character might be a source of puzzlement when they visit her grave, but the country held deep significance for Ruth. In addition to her being born there, her family worked as missionaries in China for many years. However, the meaning of this character holds much more significance than a place of birth. It shows the heart of a woman who knew her transformation was the result of the Holy Spirit. Dr. Eugene Bach, a writer for a ministry project of the Chinese church called Back to Jerusalem, talks about the character's message and gives a better understanding.

> *On her grave stone is the Chinese character for righteousness (義). It is a very special Chinese character that carries the entire Christian message in it. The Chinese character for righteousness, "yi" (義), tells a special story because it is made up of two characters—lamb (羊) + me (我). The "lamb" is on top and the character for "me" is underneath, so the Chinese message of the story in this simple Chinese character is that a lamb over me equals righteousness!*[13]

What amazes me about this epitaph is how much is stated in a few English words and one Chinese character. The sentiment expressed is a beautiful lesson for us all to remember as we journey through this life. As long as we're on this planet, our change and growth will be continuous. This growth is the result of Christ in us and our responsiveness to his Spirit. We'll never fully "arrive" on this side of heaven, and we'll need forgiveness when we falter. But thank God, he never leaves, and his faithfulness does not depend on our faultlessness.

Friend, God wants to take us to someplace new, brimming with possibility and promise. He wants to reveal a person you've yet to encounter but who is waiting to show her strength and resilience. However, we can't get there without releasing the limiting mentalities that keep us stagnant. Can you imagine what would've happened if the people we've been reading about in Scripture had refused to let go of the familiar? We wouldn't have the amazing stories we now read, filled with miracles and wonder. We wouldn't have the gift of seeing fishermen, tax collectors, and doctors transformed into teachers and writers of the gospel.

These ordinary people saw who God was and were changed. May we see who he is and be changed too.

DISCUSSION QUESTIONS

1. Have you ever tried something you didn't think you would like or be good at, but later found the exact opposite to be true? What did the experience teach you about yourself?

2. Read Luke 22:31–32. What do Jesus's words reveal about Simon's future? How does this passage encourage you?

3. Think about the person you were when you first came to know Jesus. How have you changed? Was there ever something about yourself you thought would never change, but later it did?

12

don't confuse the call with the outcome

I looked out at the large lecture room and saw eight faces looking back at me. The space was much too big for this size group, and yet here we were. Busying myself with last-minute prep, I made a conscious effort not to let my face betray my disappointment. But inside, I kept thinking, *You spent hours preparing for this? For what?* With a few minutes left until my workshop started, I chatted with the attendees and asked them how the conference was going.

Months before this writers' conference, I had prayed over the opportunity and whether to pursue it. Although it was a long drive from our home in Maryland, it would help me advance my speaking skills and make connections with others in the industry. The conference director was warm and inviting in all her correspondence with me, and the details about the budget, transportation, and speaking topics fell into place. Everything had seemed to point me toward saying yes to the event, but as

I looked out at the attendees, my expectations met a reality that was very different than I envisioned.

Have you ever been there? You pray for God's guidance in a specific area and sense his nudge to move forward. Confident of his leading, you say yes. But the more steps of obedience you take, the more you face discouragement and disillusionment. Perhaps you had a specific outcome in mind but find it unattainable. Or maybe you expect a certain amount of growth or numbers as a result of your efforts, but instead, you see results that appear small or dismal.

No matter how long we've been walking with God, we all encounter these seasons of unmet expectations. They can make us second-guess the voice of God, hesitate to move forward, or even run in the other direction. A desired outcome gives us a sense of certainty that we're headed somewhere with promise. But when we don't see the outcome we envisioned, we may assume we're not headed anywhere good. Our inner voice that desires security screams, "Retreat!" Since we don't see the fruit we want, we assume there isn't any. We forget that God alone is responsible for the fruit. Our job is to respond to him in love and faith. But hearing these words and living them are two very different things, aren't they?

Here's what I know to be true—God wired us to desire fruit. Our longing to see our efforts produce something good is not misguided or detrimental to our faith. The problem we often encounter with this longing is twofold: (1) We misunderstand how the fruit is produced, and (2) we look for the wrong types of fruit. What would it look like if we surrendered this desire for results and outcomes to him? I believe we would move forward in his plans for us with more confidence and freedom. I believe we would hold our plans a little more loosely, knowing his plans are far better than anything we could imagine for ourselves.

Remember the garden I told you about in the previous chapter? That little experiment was the first time I saw the biblical metaphors about spiritual fruit come to life in front of me. In the past, I understood them in theory, but putting my hands in the soil, watering the plants, and seeing them grow gave me new insights into the verses I'd read for years.

While there are many scriptures about spiritual fruit, one of my favorite passages is John 15. Here, Jesus is the vine, and his Father is the gardener.

> *I am the true vine, and my Father is the gardener. He cuts off every branch in me that bears no fruit, while every branch that does bear fruit he prunes so that it will be even more fruitful. You are already clean because of the word I have spoken to you. Remain in me, as I also remain in you. No branch can bear fruit by itself; it must remain in the vine. Neither can you bear fruit unless you remain in me.*
>
> *I am the vine; you are the branches. If you remain in me and I in you, you will bear much fruit; apart from me you can do nothing.* (John 15:1–5)

I'd read this scripture countless times, but as I studied it again and looked at the growth in my own garden, Jesus's words hit me in a different way.

My family and I planted seeds in the soil. We watered them and made sure they had adequate space to grow, good dirt with plenty of nutrients in it, and a location with plenty of sunlight. But we didn't produce the sunlight. While we watered beds, we didn't make the rain or create the buds on the tiny branches. With each harvest, God reminded me that my ability to influence growth was limited. Yes, I could tend to the plants and exert my best efforts to take care of them. Just as the Father did, I could cut off the branches not producing fruit and prune others to make them more fruitful. But I couldn't make the seed become a seedling and later a squash or a pepper. Some of the seeds we planted never burst through the soil, and nothing I did could change that.

In John 15, we see a similar pattern. Jesus gives us one exhortation—to abide in him. Not to run ourselves ragged worrying about the amount of fruit we're producing. Not to try to quantify our success or results in all the ways the world gives us to do this. Our number one priority is to remain in him, relying on him for our strength, direction, and worth. Anything else of importance comes behind this command and relies on whether we choose to obey it.

When I'm willing to trust God more than I trust my own plans, hopes, and dreams for the future, my faith expands like new growth reaching toward the sun.

I've heard plenty of explanations of what abiding means and how to apply this concept to our day-to-day lives. Most of them involve reading our Bibles, praying, and being part of the church body. While each of these habits is good and an integral part of our growth, I can do each of these things and still not understand what it means to abide. And trust me, I'm speaking from experience here. I've practiced all of the spiritual disciplines you can think of and still felt further from God than ever. And yet, when I've experienced growth, one thing remains consistent: a willingness to surrender what I don't understand. When I'm willing to trust God more than I trust my own plans, hopes, and dreams for the future, my faith expands like new growth reaching toward the sun.

As I look at our little garden today and ponder what it means to abide, I think of Jesus as the sun. The sun's heat and light are beyond my ability to control, and yet both are vital to each plant's existence. So instead of trying to bend the sun's rays, I plant my seeds in places where they can receive them. If I notice one crop is not getting enough of the sun's vital nutrients, I move it to a place where it can thrive. The same truth applies to you and me.

We cannot abide in a God we're trying to manipulate. Surrender, at its very core, means release. It's releasing our grip of control and reaching toward his light, even when we'd rather bury ourselves in the dirt of defeat. Neither can we abide in a God we're not near. This nearness looks like:

1. **Actively choosing to trust him, even when we don't see the outcome we want.** One way to practice this is to declare his faithfulness with our mouths, even when we don't *feel* his presence. The Psalms are filled with verses of praise and are a good place to start.
2. **Telling him about our disappointments and unmet expectations.** Often, God will use our honest confession to shift our perspective and reveal a facet of our situation we hadn't seen before. He can also mold these moments of transparency into a place of sanctuary where we experience a peace that goes beyond our circumstances.
3. **Creating space to behold his glory.** Sometimes we spend so much time talking, we forget to create time to just be. I'm raising my hand here because I'm guilty. We forget that God often speaks in the moments of stillness. Making space for these moments can allow us to encounter God in new ways.

Most of all, abiding is about intention. Friend, God knows your heart. If your heart is to love him and honor him, he knows. He sees not only your deepest desires but your deepest disappointments. Trust him with what you don't understand, and he will transform your soul.

Fruit of the Heart, Not the Hand

Transformation is what it's all about, right? As followers of Jesus, we don't want to stay where we are. And yet in this journey with him, we often misconstrue matters of the heart with matters of the hand. We want to see fruit, but sometimes we think the harvest is more physical than it actually is.

If we examine the types of fruit mentioned throughout the New Testament, most of them are not physical in nature. And when we look even closer at spiritual fruit, none of them are. Their abundance is internal and in direct correlation to the posture of our hearts. While this internal transformation can certainly affect what others see on the outside, it starts within. Fruit that will last comes from deep roots, buried in rich, life-giving soil. It comes from the choices we make in those everyday moments no one else sees.

Most of us are familiar with the fruits of the Spirit Paul writes about in Galatians: love, joy, peace, forbearance, kindness, goodness, faithfulness, gentleness, and self-control (Gal. 5:22–23). But there's a crucial aspect to each of these types of fruit, and one we may overlook. It's trust. Trust is the undercurrent of every good harvest we see when we're walking with God. Our ability to love others will be limited if we don't trust that God loved us first and can work through even hurtful situations. We won't have peace if we don't trust God's ability to move in ways we don't see and know he is faithful even in our discouragement. While trust isn't one of the fruits listed here, it is the life-giving nutrient in the soil of our lives. Isaiah 26:3 (ESV) says, "You keep him in perfect peace whose mind is stayed on you, because he trusts in you."

> As I trust God with those unmet expectations, the effect is counterintuitive—I also trust my ability to hear his voice more.

When I walked into the oversized conference room years ago and saw the sparsely filled room, I gave myself a moment to feel the disappointment and sense of failure. Even while I smiled and greeted the attendees, I acknowledged the truth—this was not what I wanted. But then, I shifted my focus to the gift in front of me. I had a class to teach, and although the class was small, women and men were there, ready to learn. Somehow, God would use those circumstances in ways I didn't understand at the time. I had to look out at the faces greeting me and say to myself, "Each person here came to this classroom for a reason, and I'm going to give them the best of me." And you know what? God brought women to that workshop whom I am still in contact with today. He knew I wasn't ready to speak in front of a huge crowd yet, and this opportunity laid the foundation I needed to gain confidence.

As I trust God with those unmet expectations, the effect is counterintuitive—I also trust my ability to hear his voice more. I realize that what I perceive as roadblocks are often an invitation to deeper faith. My disappointment is a sacred place where I can come to him with my full self, not withholding my emotions but giving them to God. And as I do this, his voice and his presence become more tangible and real. Why? Because transparency is the conduit the Spirit uses to speak to our hearts. In these moments, he reminds me, "I give them eternal life, and they shall never perish; no one will snatch them out of my hand" (John 10:28). What I perceive as a setback or a failure becomes a space for God to say, "Nothing can keep me from you. Nothing can exclude you from your place right here in my love."

Friend, trusting God is not something I do perfectly. None of us do. In all honesty, I can be quite the control freak at times, thinking my way is best and trying to keep a tight grip on things important to me. But the more I learn to release my grip and trust God with the details, the more I see the truth—he has it all under control, and he doesn't need my help. Because of his grace, he invites me to be part of the work he's doing, but his ability to carry out his plans doesn't depend on me. This truth makes me breathe a big sigh of relief and say, "Thank you, God."

Trust Takes Time

I wish I could tell you there was a magic formula where we could always be 100 percent certain we were hearing God's voice. But hearing God's voice is more like a dance than a formula. The more time we spend with him, the more we learn to let him lead. We follow his rhythm instead of trying to take over.

Trust is the soil where the fruits of the Spirit grow and thrive, but trust takes time. My husband and I tell our kids on a repeated basis, "Trust is earned." We're not going to drop our seven-year-old at a stranger's house for the night or give someone we just met the keys to our home. While God has already given us everything to earn trust, this trust is still nurtured through time. With each intentional act of abiding, noticing his faithfulness, and praising him in the middle of hardship, we create a steady story illustrating his character for us to look back on. As we look back, we see time spent with him not only in the highs and lows of life but in the middle ground. And friend, the middle ground is where we spend most seasons.

Most of us know Chip and Joanna Gaines for their successes, but recently I learned how much time this couple spent waiting. Dreams and plans God placed in their hearts didn't come to fruition at a rapid pace. Last week, I read an article in *Magnolia* magazine about how they waited for over a decade to buy a castle they'd been eying in the Waco area. The castle had been vacant for years, and they would often visit the property, walk through it, and dream about the day they might transform it. Through the delay and the tension of the in-between, they learned how crucial patience is as we pursue the passions and desires of our hearts. Joanna writes,

> *Instead of letting that time between teach and shape me, I pushed and shoved the sand through the hourglass, forgetting that so much gets worked out during the journey. Isn't that where the endless choices exist? I'm learning that we can have all sorts of endings, but we also arrive there as a different version of ourselves based on how we hold the middle.*
>
> *Call it waiting well; call it patience. For me, when I'm simply present for the in-between, that's when clarity comes into focus, when growth digs its roots. It's not a passive kind of pause but an active awareness of the weight it carries.*[1]

I love how Joanna points to clarity as one of the benefits of waiting. In the everyday journey of hearing God's voice, that's what we want, right? But as I pursue him and seek him, I also realize I can't rush it. Those moments of clarity often come in an instant—in the middle of a long walk, a shower, or a conversation—but those instances are built from the slow, uncertain minutes of waiting and patience in between. They're built on time.

Joanna also makes another key point in this quote—waiting is not passive. But we often think it is, don't we? We might conjure images of ourselves sitting on a hillside, waiting for Jesus to return. However, this is not how God wants us to spend our time. Here are some ways we can make the best of each season he gives us, whether it's a mountain top one, a valley, or the middle ground of in-between.

Make Use of the Resources He's Given You

Sometimes I can fall into the trap of thinking that because one area of my life is on hold, I must pause every other area as well. But God has given us gifts and resources for a reason. No matter what season of life we're in, we have a purpose and a reason for being there. We can love the people he's placed around us, even if it's simply through small, random acts of kindness.

Make Note of His Faithfulness in the Big and the Small Things

When we record God's faithfulness and provision, we build a timeless piece of evidence for us to look back on later. In my book *Shift*, I call these altars of remembrance. These altars will bolster our faith and trust during seasons when we face discouragement and unmet expectations.

If you're in a season where it's difficult to see God's faithfulness in the big things, record the small—a smile from a stranger, food in the fridge, or the warmth of the sun on your face.

Give the Outcomes to God. Then, Give Them to Him Again.

Surrender is another element of faith we often think is passive. But it isn't. I imagine my daughter when she's trying to carry a heavy backpack filled with more weight than her tiny frame can manage. When I offer to carry it for her, she must actively choose to give it to me. The weight doesn't shift off her shoulders simply because she says, "Here, Mom." It involves effort on her part.

In the same way, when I surrender an outcome to God, I can say, "Here, God. Please take this." But I still have to give it to him. While the shift isn't physical, it's an active change in my mindset from "I've got this" to "God, I trust you with this."

* * *

Each of these practices is a day-by-day rhythm. Some days we will do them well, and other days we won't. But thank God, we have a Good Shepherd. He chases away the wolf who comes to steal, kill, destroy, and whisper lies of "You're not good enough." Our Shepherd chases after a sheep when she follows a path he never intended for her. No one is going to snatch her or any of us away, because he laid down his life. Not part of it or a fragment of it, but all of it.

When we remember the truth, we also realize the most important outcome of any call God gives us is for us to say yes. All other outcomes are in the hands of the One who stretched them out for us all.

DISCUSSION QUESTIONS

1. Has there ever been a time when you took a step of faith in response to God's prompting, but the outcome looked completely different than you envisioned? How did you respond? How did the experience impact your faith?

2. In this chapter, we talked about how trust is the critical factor to each of the spiritual fruits mentioned in the Bible. What impact has trust had on your life and your faith? In what areas do you think God is asking you to trust him more?

3. Time is another key element to producing fruit and seeing the outcomes we desire. What do you think happens when we try to rush the process of producing fruit?

13

you have a beautiful guarantee

In my seven-year-old daughter's world, the pinky promise is the most binding of all promises. Multiple times a week, I hear her demand that her brothers make this irrevocable agreement with her. Usually, the promise involves her siblings playing a board game or video game of her choice by a certain time. Since there is a significant age difference between Elise and her brothers, they often butt heads when trying to agree on activities they can all engage in together. When Elise doesn't get her way, she invokes the pinky promise as a guarantee that she will get her choice later.

Since my sons are typical teenage and preteen boys, this promise doesn't always work out the way Elise planned. They will try to stretch out the agreement to several days or a week later instead of meeting the specified timeframe. Or they'll have something more pressing they need to do. This always results in loud whining or high-pitched screaming from the youngest female in the house. When I try to play the enforcer, I'm usually met with statements like, “I didn’t say it would be today,” or “That’s not what I said.” In less than a day, the terms have become muddled.

I used to get aggravated and lose my patience when these arguments happened. I mean, these boys know what they’re getting themselves into when they make a promise to their little sister, right? But then, with God’s guidance and plenty of grace, I began to see them as an opportunity. I realized my kids’ bickering was a chance for me to further define what a promise means and show them the difference between our promises and God’s promises.

As we’ve discussed throughout this book, my daughter’s desire for a guarantee isn’t new or unique. This longing is part of being human, with its roots in Genesis when the first man and woman were created. Sometimes this longing is fed by a selfish want and other times it isn’t, but it is a constant we will see throughout our lifetime. What struck me about Elise’s ongoing pinky promises is that while on the surface her motivation seemed self-centered, the deeper desire was not. She wanted to be with her brothers. Yes, her need to control the details was fed by self-centeredness, but her innate yearning to spend time with her siblings is a part of her designed by God.

> If I study the promises God made from Genesis all the way through Revelation, each one of them is motivated by one sole desire: God’s longing to be with you and me.

Here’s what blows my mind. If I study the promises God made from Genesis all the way through Revelation, each one of them is motivated by one sole desire: God’s longing to be with you and me. Even the promises of the law given through Moses were to point God’s people toward their need for a Redeemer and to draw them into a relationship with him. But thanks be to Jesus, you and I have a much better promise. And because of the promise God made when we declared Jesus Christ as Lord, we received a guarantee much better than a thousand pinky promises. We received a seal that declares we are his: the Holy Spirit.

Paul tells us what this seal means for us in Ephesians, saying,

> *You also were included in Christ when you heard the message of truth, the gospel of your salvation. When you believed, you were marked in him with a seal, the promised Holy Spirit, who is a deposit guaranteeing our inheritance until the redemption of those who are God's possession—to the praise of his glory.* (Eph. 1:13–14)

Did you notice the word *guarantee*? This isn't some frivolous act motivated by selfish desires or human nature. Nor is it a "You will be like God" guarantee motivated by a manipulative, deceitful heart (Gen. 3:5). This is a "You will be like and with me" guarantee made by a perfect, holy God. He is saying, "You are mine." And to make sure we understand the permanency of this promise, he placed a seal on us. He knew we would need not only a Helper in the form of the Holy Spirit but that we would need assurance of his intent. As we've discussed before, we're forgetful humans who need continual reminders of God's love and his truth. This seal is flawless evidence of his heart toward those who declare him as Lord.

When I think of a seal, I think of notaries. The seal they place on those important documents verifies they were there, in the flesh, witnessing the signature and the identity of the signers. In the same way, God is now placing his verification of our identity on us. We are no longer defined by our doubts and insecurities, but by the One who defined security by his blood.

So what does this mean for us today? How does this seal impact the way we live our day-to-day lives and how we interact with others? While the hope contained in this promise always struck me, I didn't realize until recent years its impact on today. I interpreted it as speaking of heaven only, and while grateful for its hope for the future, I didn't see these words' potential to change how I live each moment. But then, as the Spirit often does, he illuminated this passage in a whole new way, and I saw the hidden beauty I was missing.

The Guarantee of Today

Part of this beauty God revealed rests in the tense of the verbs the author uses. If we continue in Ephesians, Paul has much to say about what God has done for the church, what his purpose is, and what our position is once we receive him. But here's what stood out to me as I read about all these beautiful works of God. The verbs Paul uses are not in the future tense, as though these things will happen someday when we meet God in heaven. His emphasis here isn't the place God is preparing for me, although this is another promise we have in him. They are written in the past tense, with the emphasis on what he has *already done.* Why does this matter? Let's dig into Ephesians 2 to find out.

In chapter 2, Paul talks about the key transformation God made in us as believers and coheirs with Christ. He has transformed us from our dead selves, who followed our selfish impulses, to life in him. As we've stated before, this life is sealed by his Spirit who lives in us. And not only that, but he gave us a position at his table.

> *God raised us up with Christ and seated us with him in the heavenly realms in Christ Jesus, in order that*

> *in the coming ages he might show the incomparable riches of his grace, expressed in his kindness to us in Christ Jesus.* (Eph. 2:6–7)

Our seat with him is not something we receive as a result of reaching an exclusive level of spiritual awareness or completing items on an invisible checklist. It is already given, and this position affects not only our future but our lives in the here and now.

Heather Holleman explains this concept further in her book *Seated with Christ*:

> *I've found that living as if I'm already seated at the table purifies my motivations in my work and ministry. I'm motivated by Christ's love and not a need to belong somewhere. I'm free from self-absorption and constant self-evaluation about whether I'm enough. I'm not fighting for a place. Whether I fail or succeed against some arbitrary standard no longer matters for my identity and my heart.*[1]

Instead of fighting for her place, Holleman is resting in it. She realizes she isn't seated at the table with a frivolous God who will unfriend her on social media for making a comment he doesn't agree with. She is seated with a God who gave up his rightful position in order to give her an eternal one that she did nothing to deserve. And the good news? You and I have this same assurance.

Now, there's one distinction we need to make clear. This seat God gives us has nothing to do with material status. It is not given as a means of comparison with others or so we can achieve bragging rights. On the contrary, it has everything to do with God showing the world his kindness and grace. By taking our seat at the table and living as though we know the permanency of this place, we will create a picture for others to see the heart of God.

So how does taking this seat transform our day-to-day lives? We've discussed the verb tense Paul uses and some of the intention behind it, but these concepts may still seem ethereal and otherworldly. Let's dig into the ways this position at God's table means everything for our mindset and gives certainty to our souls today. I believe what we'll see is that this security carries over into our interactions with others, our attitude toward successes and failures, and how we respond to God's voice in faith. Here are three certainties we can rest in.

We can be certain God's heart toward us doesn't change. That seal we talked about? It's world-proof. God didn't give us a seal that fades after too much time in the sunlight or wash cycle where we didn't read the clothing label. It isn't like the seal you put on your deck to prevent the elements from damaging it, but then end up replacing the following year. His seal is permanent. If we believe this truth in our core, it will transform us from the inside out because our fear of having to measure up will be replaced by confidence in our identity. Instead of living with uncertainty about who we are or wondering if God will decide we're no longer worth it, we can claim the name he's already given us as his children.

When my middle child was a toddler, he went through a phase where if you called him anything other than his exact name, he would correct you. Since each of our kids has various nicknames, this drew quite a few chuckles from me and my husband. But Gabe didn't understand the need for any name other than his own. "I'm not a turkey; I'm Gabe!" he would say with as much seriousness as his three-year-old voice could muster.

I believe at a deep level he probably couldn't articulate at the time, my son needed to be assured of his identity. My husband and I spent a lot of time deciding on the name we would give him, and our choice wasn't the result of a flippant conversation or something we decided on a whim. We put thought into it, researching the meaning of names, saying them out loud, and discussing how they sounded with middle and last names. We chose "Gabriel" not only because of his role in the Bible as the archangel who announced Jesus's birth but also because his name means "God is my strength."

While this name is important to us, the amount of time and intention we put into my son's name is minor compared to the thought and foresight God puts into our names. In Revelation, John talks about the new name God will give those he calls his own.

> *Whoever has ears, let them hear what the Spirit says to the churches. To the one who is victorious, I will give some of the hidden manna. I will also give that person a white stone with a new name written on it, known only to the one who receives it.* (Rev. 2:17)

Throughout Scripture, we see God's heart for his people reflected in names. When a follower's faith brings a transformation into the person he created them to be, God gives him or her a new name. Abram receives the name Abraham. Sarai changes to Sarah. These new names signify belonging, and God gives you and me a new name too.

As Revelation says, this name isn't written on a scrap piece of paper or in pencil. It's written on stone. When I picture this, I see permanency. I see commitment. I don't see a God who will give up on me because I'm stuck in a season of hesitancy or doubt. And because of this assurance, my gait becomes easier. The tension in my shoulders loosens.

We can be certain our position in Christ is a result of fulfilling his plan, not ours. As Paul emphasizes throughout Ephesians, our redemption was God's plan all along. It wasn't his plan B. But God's plans aren't limited to salvation. We don't take our seat next to him and simply sit there until the second coming. There are things he wants us to do here on earth to draw others to his truth and share his love.

> *We are God's handiwork, created in Christ Jesus to do good works, which God prepared in advance for us to do.* (Eph. 2:10)

Most of us who have spent any time in the church are familiar with this scripture. It's one of the most quoted verses and for a good reason. The emphasis is often on the former part of the verse, where the word *handiwork* can also be translated as "masterpiece," from the original Greek word *poema. Poema* is Greek for poem. I mean, who doesn't like being called a poem? But here's the problem: These teachings put the emphasis on me and the other believers listening. I can almost hear my inner voice singing, "I am so great. Me, me, me."

The facet of this verse I overlooked for years, and never heard anyone talk about, is in the second half about good works. These good works are not a result of my intellect or genius. They're not even my plan. They're God's. When I carry them out, I am enacting his inspiration, creativity, and imagination, not mine. Yes, he gives this inspiration as a gift and desires for me to use it, but the genesis of this gift is always the Creator. Why does this matter? Because knowing this takes the pressure off me. Instead of obsessing about results and being anxious about everything going according to my agenda, my focus is on the One who cannot fail.

We can be certain that if the outcome isn't good, God isn't finished yet. It's important to note the adjective Paul uses to describe these works God planned for us to do. He tells us they're good. But because our focus tends to be on finite results, we may not see the good right away. If we don't reach a goal we had in mind or we receive a disappointing response from others involved, we may conclude our efforts weren't worth the time. This mindset can cause us to become stuck or even quit an endeavor where God is still working. We may think we didn't hear him after all and his prompting was a figment of our imagination. And this is exactly what our enemy wants.

In order to persevere in the good works God planned for us to do, it's crucial for us to realize that God's pace is not our pace.

In order to persevere in the good works God planned for us to do, it's crucial for us to realize that God's pace is not our pace. The growth and fruit we long to see are often slow in coming. These works we're doing don't have pie charts or statistics on Excel sheets but are being realized in the hearts and minds of others around us. Our aim is to transform lives, not data, but the fruit is not always evident. The seeds are germinating beneath the soil and absorbing the nutrients they need to break forth into the sunlight. Jennifer Dukes Lee describes this process in her book *Growing Slow*.

> *Stories of spectacular growth in businesses or ministries earn accolades and trophies at banquets for the Who's Who and the so-and-so's. But how are unseen and internal milestones rewarded? Probably less like*

> *a framed certificate and more like a "prize for which God has called me heavenward in Christ Jesus."*[2]

Sometimes, we won't see the fruit we desire in this lifetime. But we can be sure if the word we received was from God, it will not return void. It will accomplish what he intended, regardless of what we do or don't see. This is the certainty we have when we move forward in faith in God's will: The outcome will always be good because he is good.

Beyond the Pinky Promise

My daughter's pinky promises aren't reserved for her brothers. Sometimes, she requests them from Dad and Mom too. These promises can involve anything from dinner plans to visits to see her grandparents. Because I want her to know my word isn't something I give in a flippant way, I almost always deliver on whatever it is I've promised. But every now and then, life happens. Circumstances beyond my control happen and I have to explain the nature of these promises to my daughter, that they are bound by factors we can't always predict. She has an opportunity to learn how to deal with disappointment, and I can help her navigate it.

Several weeks ago, there was an unexpected change to our schedule, and we had one of these conversations. My daughter is still learning about the unpredictability of life, but she responded to the situation with plenty of grace and an optimistic outlook. In the world of parenting first-grade girls, it was a win in my book. But after the conversation, I realized something even more encouraging.

God's promises aren't bound by those unpredictable factors beyond our control. Because he is omniscient and omnipresent, he sees every contingency and roadblock. He sees the beginning and the end, and everything in between. He is certain of our future because it was his plan and his promise, not ours. So when we encounter those interruptions to our best intentions and those unforeseen detours, we can be sure God knows. He is not surprised. And his promise to stay with us through what may seem like a plan B does not change.

The Promise Is to Move You Forward

Throughout this book, we've been unpacking three promises Jesus gives in John 10 and have spent the last three chapters diving into the final one: No one will snatch his sheep out of his hand. This means no forces of darkness or creation in the past, present, or future have the ability to separate us from God or his love (Rom. 8:38–39). Now, here's what I want you to remember: One of the biggest ways the Enemy keeps us stuck is by convincing us that he *can* snatch us out of God's hand. He tries to make us believe he has more power than he actually does. One of his tactics for doing this is by convincing us there is a plan B and shifting our focus toward ourselves. He knows that when our focus is on ourselves, we will only see our shortcomings.

On the contrary, when we shift our focus toward God and the promise he gives us, our feet will be propelled forward. This perspective reminds us Jesus never leaves his pasture, and no one can climb in or enter through any other way but the door, Jesus himself. This door is the key to all life, fullness, purpose, and love. It is a door guarded against any force of darkness trying to enter through it.

Friend, if you've entered through this door, it is the only door you will ever need to walk through to find true, lasting certainty. This is a promise you can stand on. It is everything. As you hear his voice and move in his pasture, you can be sure he will give you all that you need. And you can be certain that as you respond to his voice, he will guide you with his love.

DISCUSSION QUESTIONS

1. Read Revelation 2:17. What does the fact that God writes your new name on a stone tablet mean to you? How does this verse change your perspective about the uncertainties of life?

2. One of the certainties we have in this life is that God's heart toward us won't change. How can remembering this promise help you take a step of faith that God is prompting you to take, even when it seems scary?

3. While life is unpredictable, God's character is not. What are some aspects of God's character that have encouraged you when you've been tempted to worry about the unknown?

acknowledgments

The more I write, the more I learn that no writer can create alone. This book was five years in the making, and I would never have finished it without the support of friends, family, and colleagues along the way.

Thank you to Chris for always being my biggest fan and faithfully reminding me where my help comes from. I know you're still holding out for me to become the sugar mama you always hoped for. Maybe one day I will give you your wish.

Thank you to my kids—Jaden, Gabe, and Elise—for teaching me what it means to have a childlike faith, for showing me his love each and every day, and for inspiring me in more ways than you know. I am so grateful to be your mom and for the opportunity to see you grow.

Thank you to my agent, Blythe Daniel. Your heart for writers is a gift to everyone who has the opportunity to meet you. You believed in the message of this book and helped to make sure it found its place in the publishing world.

Thank you to Kristine, Lyli, Kristi, and Lisa for being my dear friends, my prayer warriors, and some of my greatest supporters. Our Zoom calls and Voxer chats were a lifeline to me throughout this process, and you were always there to remind me of what mattered most.

To Jason Fikes and the entire team at Leafwood, thank you for being such a wonderful team to work with. Thank you for believing in the message of this book and seeing the need for it.

To my parents, thank you for your faithful prayers, encouragement, and steadfast love. You show me every day what it looks like to love without limits.

To my brother, Daniel—years ago you encouraged me to write when I didn't see a way. I've never forgotten that.

To my church family at LOH, I love doing life with you and am so grateful for your continual encouragement and support.

To Shelby, Glynnis, and the entire team at Proverbs 31 Ministries, you care for your writers so well. I love not only being a part of your ministry but on a team who truly cares for each person's needs.

Most of all, thank you to God. You are my life, my breath, and the reason I wake up each morning with hope. You are the reason for each word in this book. Thank you for loving me with all-consuming love.

about the author

Abby McDonald is wife to Chris and the mom to three children. After moving around the country several times, her family settled in western Maryland, where they enjoy the small-town life, mountains, and camping. She is active in ministry at her church and writes regularly for numerous publications, including Proverbs 31 Ministries. She is also a writing coach and developmental editor, and she loves to help other writers pursue their God-given dreams.

Abby writes regularly on her website, abbymcdonald.org, and is known for her transparency and cut-to-the-heart-of-the-matter style as she encourages her readers to embrace their unique, God-given identity and follow him in faith. She proclaims the truth that none of us are too far from God; he pursues each one of us with the heart of a Father chasing after his child.

notes

CHAPTER ONE

[1]William Paul Young, *The Shack: Where Tragedy Confronts Eternity* (Windblown Media, 2007), 191.

CHAPTER TWO

[1]Madeleine L'Engle, *Walking on Water: Reflections on Faith and Art* (WaterBrook, 1980; repr. 2001), 71.

CHAPTER THREE

[1]*Merriam-Webster Dictionary*, s.v. "desire," accessed September 25, 2024, https://www.merriam-webster.com/dictionary/desire.

[2]Daniel L. Akin, "desire," in *Baker's Evangelical Dictionary of Biblical Theology*, ed. Walter A. Elwell (Baker, 1996), accessed on Bible Study Tools, https://www.biblestudytools.com/dictionary/desire/.

[3]Emily P. Freeman, *The Next Right Thing: A Simple Soulful Practice for Making Life's Decisions* (Revell, 2019), 90.

[4]"8378. Taavah," Bible Hub, accessed September 26, 2024, https://biblehub.com/hebrew/8378.htm.

CHAPTER FOUR

[1]Jennifer Tucker, *Breath as Prayer: Calm Your Anxiety, Focus Your Mind, and Renew Your Soul* (Thomas Nelson, 2022), 20, 21, 29.

CHAPTER FIVE

[1]Randy Payne, "LOH Missions // East Africa," interview with Tim McGregor, church service, July 24, 2022, by Lighthouse of Hope Church, @LOHChurch, YouTube, https://www.youtube.com/live/wc7pLVKuiIE.

[2]Adam Clarke, "Commentary on John 10:9," *The New Testament of Our Lord and Saviour Jesus Christ: The Text . . . with a Commentary and Critical Notes,* Clarke's Commentary vol. 5, New Testament vol. 1: *Matthew to the Acts* (Abingdon-Cokesbury, 1831), 592, read at https://www.studylight.org/commentaries/eng/acc/john-10.html.

CHAPTER SIX

[1]Oswald Chambers, "The Graciousness of Uncertainty," *My Utmost for His Highest,* April 29, 2024, https://utmost.org/classic/the-graciousness-of-uncertainty-classic/.

CHAPTER SEVEN

[1]"Turkish Sheep Die in 'Mass Jump,'" BBC News, July 8, 2005, http://news.bbc.co.uk/2/hi/europe/4665511.stm.

[2]Craig S. Keener, "Jesus Reveals Himself as a Disciple of God, Not of the Rabbis (7:14–24)," *The IVP Bible Background Commentary: New Testament* (InterVarsity Press, 2014), accessed on BibleGateway, https://www.biblegateway.com/resources/ivp-nt/Jesus-Reveals-Himself-Disciple.

CHAPTER EIGHT

[1]Lisa Whittle, *God Knows: When Your Worries and Whys Need More Than Temporary Relief* (Thomas Nelson, 2023), 35.

CHAPTER NINE

[1]Tyler Staton, *Praying Like Monks, Living Like Fools: An Invitation to the Wonder and Mystery of Prayer* (Thomas Nelson, 2022), 79, italics original.

CHAPTER TEN

[1]"The Unique Connection – Pandora," posted on April 21, 2015, by Siingh 'Food & Fitness,' @adsstocker, YouTube, https://www.youtube.com/watch?v=90UErVF5LHQ.

[2]Curt Thompson, *The Soul of Shame: Retelling the Stories We Believe about Ourselves* (InterVarsity Press, 2015), 13.

CHAPTER ELEVEN

[1]Oswald Chambers, *Our Brilliant Heritage / If You Will Be Perfect / Disciples Indeed: The Inheritance for God's Transforming Mind and Heart* (Our Daily Bread, 2015), 138.

[2]David C. McCasland, "End of Construction," Our Daily Bread, September 14, 2008, https://odb.org/2008/09/14/end-of-construction.

[3]Eugene Bach, "Billy Graham's Wife's Gravestone Tells a Chinese Story that Few Know About," Back to Jerusalem, March 3, 2021, https://backtojerusalem.com/billy-grahams-wifes-grave-stone-tells-a-chinese-story-that-few-know-about/.

CHAPTER TWELVE

[1]Joanna Gaines, "Worth the Weight," *Magnolia*, Spring 2023, https://magnolia.com/blog/article/441209/a-note-from-jo-on-patience/.

CHAPTER THIRTEEN

[1]Heather Holleman, *Seated with Christ: Living Freely in a Culture of Comparison* (Moody, 2015), 30.

[2]Jennifer Dukes Lee, *Growing Slow: Lessons on* Un-Hurrying *Your Heart from an Accidental Farm Girl* (Zondervan, 2021), 30–31.